Police and Policing

CRIME, JUSTICE, AND PUNISHMENT

Police and Policing

Sandy Asirvatham

Austin Sarat, GENERAL EDITOR

CHELSEA HOUSE PUBLISHERS
Philadelphia

Chelsea House Publishers

Editor-in-Chief Sally Cheney
Director of Production Kim Shinners
Production Manager Pamela Loos
Art Director Sara Davis

Staff for POLICE AND POLICING

Senior Editor John Ziff
Associate Art Director Takeshi Takahashi
Production Editor Bonnie Cohen
Cover Designer Keith Trego

First Printing

1 3 5 7 9 8 6 4 2

The Chelsea House World Wide Web address is
http://www.chelseahouse.com

Library of Congress Cataloging-in-Publication Data
applied for.
ISBN: 0-7910-4301-0

Contents

CRIME, JUSTICE, AND PUNISHMENT

Fears and Fascinations:

An Introduction to Crime, Justice, and Punishment

By Austin Sarat

We live with crime and images of crime all around us. Crime evokes in most of us a deep aversion, a feeling of profound vulnerability, but it also evokes an equally deep fascination. Today, in major American cities the fear of crime is a major fact of life, some would say a disproportionate response to the realities of crime. Yet the fear of crime is real, palpable in the quickened steps and furtive glances of people walking down darkened streets. At the same time, we eagerly follow crime stories on television and in movies. We watch with a "who done it" curiosity, eager to see the illicit deed done, the investigation undertaken, the miscreant brought to justice and given his just deserts. On the streets the presence of crime is a reminder of our own vulnerability and the precariousness of our taken-for-granted rights and freedoms. On television and in the movies the crime story gives us a chance to probe our own darker motives, to ask "Is there a criminal within?" as well as to feel the collective satisfaction of seeing justice done.

Fear and fascination, these two poles of our engagement with crime, are, of course, only part of the story. Crime is, after all, a major social and legal problem, not just an issue of our individual psychology. Politicians today use our fear of, and fascination with, crime for political advantage. How we respond to crime, as well as to the political uses of the crime issue, tells us a lot about who we are as a people as well as what we value and what we tolerate. Is our response compassionate or severe? Do we seek to understand or to punish, to enact an angry vengeance or to rehabilitate and welcome the criminal back into our midst? The CRIME, JUSTICE, AND PUNISHMENT series is designed to explore these themes, to ask why we are fearful and fascinated, to probe the meanings and motivations of crimes and criminals and of our responses to them, and, finally, to ask what we can learn about ourselves and the society in which we live by examining our responses to crime.

Crime is always a challenge to the prevailing normative order and a test of the values and commitments of law-abiding people. It is sometimes a Raskolnikov-like act of defiance, an assertion of the unwillingness of some to live according to the rules of conduct laid out by organized society. In this sense, crime marks the limits of the law and reminds us of law's all-too-regular failures. Yet sometimes there is more desperation than defiance in criminal acts; sometimes they signal a deep pathology or need in the criminal. To confront crime is thus also to come face-to-face with the reality of social difference, of class privilege and extreme deprivation, of race and racism, of children neglected, abandoned, or abused whose response is to enact on others what they have experienced themselves. And occasionally crime, or what is labeled a criminal act, represents a call for justice, an appeal to a higher moral order against the inadequacies of existing law.

Figuring out the meaning of crime and the motivations of criminals and whether crime arises from defiance, desperation, or the appeal for justice is never an easy task. The motivations and meanings of crime are as varied as are the persons who engage in criminal conduct. They are as mysterious as any of the mysteries of the human soul. Yet the desire to know the secrets of crime and the criminal is a strong one, for in that knowledge may lie one step on the road to protection, if not an assurance of one's own personal safety. Nonetheless, as strong as that desire may be, there is no available technology that can allow us to know the whys of crime with much confidence, let alone a scientific certainty. We can, however, capture something about crime by studying the defiance, desperation, and quest for justice that may be associated with it. Books in the CRIME, JUSTICE, AND PUNISHMENT series will take up that challenge. They tell stories of crime and criminals, some famous, most not, some glamorous and exciting, most mundane and commonplace.

This series will, in addition, take a sober look at American criminal justice, at the procedures through which we investigate crimes and identify criminals, at the institutions in which innocence or guilt is determined. In these procedures and institutions we confront the thrill of the chase as well as the challenge of protecting the rights of those who defy our laws. It is through the efficiency and dedication of law enforcement that we might capture the criminal; it is in the rare instances of their corruption or brutality that we feel perhaps our deepest betrayal. Police, prosecutors, defense lawyers, judges, and jurors administer criminal justice and in their daily actions give substance to the guarantees of the Bill of Rights. What is an adversarial system of justice? How does it work? Why do we have it? Books in the CRIME, JUSTICE, AND PUNISHMENT series will examine the thrill of the chase as we seek to capture the criminal. They will also reveal the drama and majesty of the criminal trial as well as the day-to-day reality of a criminal justice system in which trials are the exception and negotiated pleas of guilty are the rule.

When the trial is over or the plea has been entered, when we have separated the innocent from the guilty, the moment of punishment has arrived. The injunction to punish the guilty, to respond to pain inflicted by inflicting pain, is as old as civilization itself. "An eye for an eye and a tooth for a tooth" is a biblical reminder that punishment must measure pain for pain. But our response to the criminal must be better than and different from the crime itself. The biblical admonition, along with the constitutional prohibition of "cruel and unusual punishment," signals that we seek to punish justly and to be just not only in the determination of who can and should be punished, but in how we punish as well. But neither reminder tells us what to do with the wrongdoer. Do we rape the rapist, or burn the home of the arsonist? Surely justice and decency say no. But, if not, then how can and should we punish? In a world in which punishment is neither identical to the crime nor an automatic response to it, choices must be made and we must make them. Books in the CRIME, JUSTICE, AND PUNISHMENT series will examine those choices and the practices, and politics, of punishment. How do we punish and why do we punish as we do? What can we learn about the rationality and appropriateness of today's responses to crime by examining our past and its responses? What works? Is there, and can there be, a just measure of pain?

CRIME, JUSTICE, AND PUNISHMENT brings together books on some of the great themes of human social life. The books in this series capture our fear and fascination with crime and examine our responses to it. They remind us of the deadly seriousness of these subjects. They bring together themes in law, literature, and popular culture to challenge us to think again, to think anew, about subjects that go to the heart of who we are and how we can and will live together.

*   *   *   *   *

At the forefront and on the front line, police play a crucial—and highly visible—role in America's criminal justice system. They receive ample public attention, especially when one of their number goes bad. Moreover, police are caught between two, at times contradictory, demands: respect the law and maintain order.

Police and Policing captures these tensions as it explores both the history and contemporary context of the work of these important law enforcement professionals. Indeed this book explores what it means for society to think of the police through the lens of professionalism. This book shows how professionalism exists in some conflict with the tendency toward militarization and how militarization is one response to the dangers of policing. Calling attention to such pressing contemporary issues as police brutality and community policing, this book is an engaging and important contribution to public understanding and debate.

GOOD COP, BAD COP

1

He is not the police officer who killed an unarmed man on the West Side last month. He is not the officer who tortured a man in a Brooklyn precinct station house three years ago. He did not shoot a squeegee man in the Bronx, frequent a Midtown brothel, run a drug ring from his locker or do anything else to tarnish the badge that he keeps on a chain around his neck.

He is Officer Eddie Vasquez, and most likely you have never heard of him.

—from "Branded by the Badge: An
Officer in a Hostile City,"
in the *New York Times*, April 2, 2000

At the close of the 20th century, the role of police officers in an increasingly violent American society has become a crucial issue for social and political debate. It seems nearly impossible to turn on the nightly television news without

Demonstrators in Los Angeles protest police brutality and racial profiling. Given the difficult nature of law enforcement and the existence of a proportion of bad cops, some conflict between the police and the communities they are charged with serving appears inevitable.

13

hearing about yet another incident of police brutality, corruption, or racism in one city or another. And while fact-based media stories paint a harsh and sometimes frightening portrait of American law enforcement, fictional narratives—a never-ending supply of cop dramas such as *Homicide*, *Law & Order*, or *NYPD Blue*—continue to glamorize police work, providing a very distorted picture of the occupation under the guise of "gritty realism."

In reality, police work is both more mundane and more broadly demanding an occupation than most cop dramas reveal. In reality, the vast majority of modern police officers are probably far more honorable, responsible, and judicious than their few peers who make news headlines with bad behavior. Although it was not always this way, modern law enforcement work has become like most other human endeavors in that it attracts different kinds of people: some of them heroically brave, good, and strong; some of them sadistic or authoritarian or morally weak; most of them decent, fair, hardworking, and pleasantly average in most ways, despite their highly specialized training and work experience.

The newspaper article quoted at the beginning of this chapter was written during a time when New York City's police force had one of the worst reputations in recent history—arguably for good reasons. Under the aegis of Mayor Rudolph Giuliani—a former prosecutor and a Republican who had won election in this majority-Democrat city with his strong "law and order" political platform—New York's cops had adopted a very tough stance toward even minor criminal activity. In part, Giuliani had been inspired by the so-called "broken window" approach to crime prevention. This concept, promoted and popularized by Harvard researchers James Q. Wilson and George Kelling in the 1980s, focused on the idea that the evidence of community deterioration—

Mayor Rudy Giuliani of New York City campaigned on a get-tough-on-crime platform. His no-tolerance policies have reduced annoyances like panhandling and graffiti but have created negative feelings in the minority community.

everything from broken windows and graffiti to panhandlers and public drunks—was itself a gateway to further deterioration and more serious criminal activity. Their proposed solution (which New York and other jurisdictions put into effect in the 1980s and 1990s) was to increase police foot-patrol presence and to establish no-tolerance policies for such relatively minor public annoyances as drug addicts, drunks, beggars, prostitutes, loiterers, and rowdy teenagers.

In New York, the efficacy of such a policy was soon evident in places such as Times Square, once a haven for drug dealers and pornographers, and now a clean, bright tourist destination for shopping and family-oriented entertainment. But many people—particularly the city's lower-income and minority communities who lived outside the paths of most tourists—felt that the police were

Using the so-called broken
windows approach to law
enforcement, New York
City police helped transform
Times Square from a center
for drug dealing, prostitu-
tion, and pornography
(below) to a family-fun
tourist destination (above).

abusing their newly reinforced powers, harassing citizens with little or no provocation, targeting blacks and Hispanics without sufficient cause, and in general behaving like bullies. A number of high-profile criminal cases, all involving police perpetrators, seemed to prove this point of view: the torture of Abner Louima in a city precinct office, the killing of Amadou Diallo by officers who mistook his wallet for a gun, the senseless deadly assault of Patrick Dorismond by a hotheaded off-duty cop.

The Louima and Diallo cases, in particular, continued to have social and political repercussions throughout New York City but also throughout the nation, even years later. In August 1997, 30-year-old Abner Louima—a recent Haitian immigrant who worked as a security guard—was arrested for fighting outside a nightclub. He claimed to have been attempting to break up a fight between two women. Louima was taken to the police precinct house, where at least one and possibly as many as four officers were involved in brutalizing him: they handcuffed him, beat him, pulled his pants down, then sodomized him with the handle of a bathroom plunger, rupturing his small intestine and damaging his bladder. He survived the attack and brought charges against the officers, most notably a 25-year-old officer named Justin Volpe. In all the press coverage and the trials that dragged on for months and even years after the incident, many of the details of that night—including the truth of exactly which officers were involved—grew murky and open to debate, and there were even some instances in which Louima himself was caught telling lies or at least embellishing the truth. (For example, early reports of the incident mentioned that the officers had shoved the handle of the plunger into Louima's mouth, knocking out his teeth; it was later revealed that Louima had lost those teeth prior to the attack and was wearing dentures when it happened.)

Nonetheless, given the evidence, it was clear that Officer Volpe and at least some of his colleagues had engaged in an outrageous and disgusting assault when they brought Louima into police custody. Justin Volpe eventually pled guilty to the crime and was sentenced to 30 years in prison, but he never apologized to or even acknowledged Louima in his public statements. His partner and two other officers were also charged in the incident and put in jail, although one of them, Charles Schwarz, maintained he was innocent of the charges and had not even been in the station house at the time of the incident.

The Amadou Diallo case was not marred by lies and inconsistencies as the Louima case had been, but it still raised grave questions regarding the way New York City police officers do their work. In February 1999, a West African immigrant living in the Bronx was shot to death by four white police officers who mistook him for an alleged rapist. The officers later testified in court that Diallo had been acting suspiciously when they approached him—looking around nervously and backing into the vestibule of an apartment building as if he didn't want to be seen. One of the officers, Sean Carroll, saw Diallo reach for his pocket to remove a black object, which Carroll took to be a gun. Believing Diallo was about to fire a gun at his partner, Carroll began shooting. All four officers emptied their guns into Diallo, discharging 41 bullets total, 19 of which hit their mark. Diallo was pinned to the wall as the bullets entered his body. Sean Carroll testified that he first thought Diallo must have been wearing a bulletproof vest—for how else would he remain standing under such heavy fire? But the man slumped down dead as soon as the barrage of bullets ended. When the officers approached the body, they realized their mistake: Diallo had been pulling his wallet out of his pocket, probably in an attempt to identify himself to the police.

The officers involved had been part of an elite Street Crime Unit that patrolled the poorest neighborhoods in New York. The SCU, whose motto was "We Own the Night," had been tremendously successful by some standards. Although they represented less than 2 percent of the overall police force, they were responsible for more than 20 percent of the city's gun arrests and had confiscated over 2,000 illegal weapons during 1997 and 1998. But some would argue that this success came at a huge cost to civil liberties, namely the freedom of law-abiding citizens to go about their lives without undue police harassment. From 1997 to 1998, SCU officers stopped and searched 45,000 men, mostly African American and Hispanic, but made only 9,000 arrests.

Abner Louima was brutalized by New York City policemen in a case that received worldwide attention. Critics cite the Louima case as a graphic illustration of how no-tolerance policing encourages police officers to behave like bullies.

The criminal trial against the officers who killed Diallo was moved out of New York City to the state capital of Albany, a predominantly white jurisdiction known for its fervent support of police officers. All four officers were acquitted of any wrongdoing in Diallo's death—a verdict that only further polarized the citizens of New York City.

Both the Louima and Diallo cases raised thorny questions regarding the training, procedures, and attitudes of police officers. Were the white officers involved simply racists who believed they were justified to behave overzealously when dealing with racial minorities? Was the real problem the fact that officers felt so pressured by the violence around them that they acted out with an exaggerated level of force when confronted with possible threats to their own lives? Or was it all just a matter of improper or rushed training? (The SCU, for example, had expanded from 150 to 400 officers almost overnight, leaving little time for thorough training.)

The "ultimate truth" of these cases will probably be debated for many years to come. But one thing seems clear: the police officers involved, whether they were sociopaths in blue or simply average cops who made grievous errors, rendered an already difficult job even tougher for New York's so-called finest, people like Officer Eddie Vasquez. Decent, hardworking cops—the city's appointed helpers and protectors, men and women who put their lives on the line, every day, on behalf of absolute strangers—were now subject to the general public's hatred, anger, and mistrust.

Although New York's struggles represented a unique moment in the development of the city and of American society in general, they were also part of the larger historical narrative of law enforcement in this country—a narrative that reveals an ongoing, fundamental tension between the "good cop" and "bad cop" aspects of the institution. Even in a democracy such as ours, the police have been granted a great deal of power over the life, death, movement, safety, privacy, and freedom of ordinary citizens. And power, as the 19th-century English historian Lord Acton pointed out, tends to corrupt. At any one point in time, there will always be some police officers who use the power of their position in legitimate, appropriate, and productive ways, along with others who have been tempted to use their power to gain unfair advantages or to exploit, oppress, or destroy those less powerful.

Related to the good cop/bad cop dichotomy is a concept that sociologist Jerome Skolnick has identified as the "law and order" dilemma. An analysis of policing in democratic society shows that the two principal purposes of the police—to enforce laws and to maintain social order—are often in conflict with one another. "As functionaries charged with maintaining order, [the police] are part of the bureaucracy" of a democracy, Skolnick wrote in his 1966 study *Justice Without Trial*. "The ideology of democratic bureaucracy emphasizes initiative rather than disciplined adherence to rules and regulations. By contrast, the rule of law emphasizes the rights of individual citizens and constraints upon the initiative of legal officials." In other words, the effectiveness of police—their ability to keep the peace and guard over a stable, orderly, safe society—is not necessarily related to how closely they abide by the law.

The difficulty of doing both parts of the job—enforcing order while respecting the established legal rights of other citizens, even if they are suspected criminals—is well dramatized in a 1991 memoir by Paul Ragonese, who was the most highly decorated police officer in New York City history. If his book, *The Soul of a Cop*, is to be trusted, Officer Ragonese is clearly a prime candidate for the label of good cop. Ragonese, or "Rags" as he's known to his cop buddies, is law-abiding, brave, and genuinely motivated by the idea of helping

In the early 1970s, Frank Serpico (above) exposed widespread police corruption in New York City. Since then, periodic scandals have come to light in American cities from Philadelphia to Los Angeles.

people and saving lives. As a Catholic boy, he wanted to become a priest, but didn't think he could go through life without marrying or having children. Instead he became a cop, but a compassionate, priestly sort of cop—the kind who was deeply proud to talk a potential suicide out of his desperate act; the kind who refused to kick a poor woman with eight children out into the street on a cold winter night, even though the landlord had ordered her evicted for not paying her rent; the kind who risked his own life to stay by the side of a woman who'd been pinned under a 35-ton crane and who would die shortly.

Rags even took it upon himself to protect a criminal suspect from another officer who planned on beating the guy up. Officer Ragonese had arrested a man named Jorge Guzman, who'd mugged an off-duty cop, and taken him into the "cage," the holding cell at the precinct. A little while later another officer, a bully and drunk named Mickey Flynn, went down to the cage and attacked Guzman, screaming that anyone who dared touch a cop deserved what he had coming. "Flynn, who was casting a huge shadow over Guzman, reached out and snatched open the cage door. He lunged inside and clamped his hands around Guzman's throat. I jumped up, ran into the cage, and pulled Flynn off, then shoved the fat slob outside and closed the door."

In recalling the incident for his book, Ragonese didn't discuss his actions at any great length, other than to describe his words to Flynn at the time: "The guy fought in the street, lost, and surrendered. The fight's over . . . I ain't gonna let no fat drunk smack my prisoner." To Ragonese, his intervention requires no larger explanation. The wheels of justice were in motion, the police had done their job in apprehending a criminal, the law would be upheld, and that was the end of the story.

Flynn, you can imagine, was motivated by other sorts of considerations. He felt called to respond with violence to what he saw as a "threat" to police authority—a man who'd unwittingly mugged a cop. Flynn was, you might say, willing to break the law in order to teach the mugger a lesson about respecting the badge. In this attitude, Flynn echoed a long line of cops throughout history, for whom the maintenance of order and the reinforcement of police authority were ultimately more important than behaving in a legal or ethical manner.

Overall, law enforcement agencies at different periods of time and in different locations may be more or less brutal, more or less corrupt, more or less organized, more or less effective at preventing and solving crimes, more or less respected by the people they set out to protect. In the early 1970s, for example, New York City police officer Frank Serpico went to the press with the story of widespread corruption on the force. A six-month investigation by the *New York Times*, and a subsequent mayoral committee investigation, revealed some shocking findings. More than 50 percent of the city's 29,600 police officers had participated in some form of corrupt practices, such as accepting regular

Life on the Beat, Part 1

You can get some sense of a cop's topsy-turvy working life by visiting one of the numerous Internet sites now run by police officers who are happy to share stories with vicarious-thrill-seeking civilians. There's even one web site (*www.lifeonthebeat.com*) where you can sign up to receive E-mail "dispatches," once or twice a week, from a cop named Russell—no last name or location given. His missives show the wide variety of calls Russell must respond to—everything from mediating arguments between next-door neighbors to handling the scene of a suicide. But as with most beat cops in America today, a huge percentage of Russell's work involves traffic stops. On a weekend in March 2000, Russell wrote about stopping a car for equipment violations (for example, a nonworking rear brake light). "The driver seemed very nice, but I could tell that . . . he was not being totally honest with me. After he handed [over his license, registration, and insurance information], I looked it over and noticed that his insurance was expired about 6 months ago. When I asked him about it, he said that he just got new insurance yesterday and accidentally left that information at home."

Russell didn't quite believe the guy, but was willing to give him the benefit of the doubt—that is, until he used his car radio to check out the driver's information. He then found out that the man had been denied a driver's license by the state, that he had no insurance, and also that there was a warrant for the man's arrest in a neighboring town. Russell handcuffed the man, who immediately started "crying like a little kid . . . sobbing and gasping." It turned out he'd been stealing credit cards. "During the booking process I located a credit card that did not belong to him. He gave 2 or 3 stories about why he had someone else's credit card. I contacted the owner of the card and he explained that the card was lost."

hush-money payments from illegal gambling establishments or drug dealers, who then remained conveniently immune to arrests or criminal prosecutions. But by the time the commission report was released in 1972, a new police commissioner had already instituted many reforms, and New York's mayor at the time, John V. Lindsay, asserted with confidence that such problems would not recur.

Lindsay, of course, had no way of knowing this for sure. Furthermore, although one agency had apparently solved or at least minimized its corruption problem at

Russell was then thrown for a loop by the owner of the credit card, who told him that he had just found a new religion, and that this particular faith had taught him to forgive the thief. The credit card owner refused to press charges, and Russell was forced to let the suspect go. "While I can see the good intentions of the card owner, my experience tells me that this suspect will not change his actions because someone forgave him. I am quite sure that I will see this suspect again."

Russell's stories show all the usual characteristics of cop tales: the cynicism, the unflappability, the dry, off-handed humor. But they also show his compassion for suffering human beings. He is, no doubt, one of the "good" ones. After a particularly slow week, Russell had one very harrowing night in early April 2000. He was called by paramedics to a house where a 27-year-old man was found in his bedroom, dead with a bullet in his brain. "What I saw next was something that I pray most people never see. The scene was so bad that most movies never show something so terrible. The man was laying on his right side on a pool of blood. The blood was very thick. The color was deep, dark, red—it was almost black." Russell had to examine the man to determine where the gunshot wound was, to try to rule this case as a homicide or suicide. As is often the case with gunshot suicides, the gun was found underneath the body. Russell, along with the medical examiner and the police sergeant who'd arrived later on the scene, ruled it a "self-inflicted, single, shot to the head." Russell then had the unenviable task of telling the family. These poor people had been in deep denial. Some of them, who'd heard the noise of the gun and then seen the body, hoped that the young man had simply tripped and struck his head loudly. "Some of the family was very well composed, but some others were sobbing and weeping uncontrollably," Russell reports.

When Russell got home, he got into the shower and stayed there until he'd used up all the hot water. "I still had the smell of that body stuck in my nostrils," he reveals. "I still had the thought of that family in my head. I heard the father blaming himself over and over.

It was a tough call."

one point in history, there was no guarantee that other jurisdictions would learn from New York's lessons. In early 2000, news broke of corrupt practices in certain Los Angeles Police Department precincts, a pattern of bad behavior that was soon being labeled the worst corruption case in history. The LAPD, already tarnished by a decade of accusations that it was a breeding ground for racist cops who enjoyed using excessive force against black and Hispanic suspects, now had to face allegations that some of its officers were stealing drugs, planting evidence, making false arrests, and covering up unjustified shootings.

Cynics and pessimists will be tempted to look at the LAPD scandal as merely one tip of one particular iceberg in a vast sea of wrongdoing—as one bad situation that luckily has been brought to light, while so many other comparable situations remain out of the public's perception. More optimistic observers will want to argue that such cases are newsworthy precisely because they represent a deviation from the norm. Historians and sociologists will eventually come to judge this particular era of law enforcement in light of the overall development of American policing and its connection to broader societal patterns.

Meanwhile, the Officer Paul Ragoneses and Officer Eddie Vasquezes of the world—the good cops, however many or few there are, who comport themselves with honor and integrity, who spend their days doing everything from getting drunk drivers off the road to aiding lost tourists to restraining wife-beaters to busting narcotics dealers, who know that each shift brings the possibility of their own violent death—are once again on the defensive, trying to do their tough job in the face of

public criticism, antagonism, and anger, and occasionally finding themselves caught in the conflict between
"law" and "order."

> [Officer Eddie Vasquez] said he understands the outcry
> when an Amadou Diallo or a Patrick Dorismond is killed
> by the police: the need to mourn, the demand for respect.
> He does not apologize for or explain away the actions of
> officers like Justin Volpe, who so brutalized Abner Louima
> three years ago. But why, he asked, does Eddie Vasquez pay
> the consequences? Why don't people see that he is one of
> the good ones, one of the many who do a difficult and
> sometimes dangerous job as best they can?

VIGILANTES AND BULLIES, HEROES AND PROFESSIONALS

2

Societies have required some form of policing for a very long time—but not quite forever. One broad-brush way to look at the development of policing is through an analysis of so-called formal and informal methods of social control.

Formal law enforcement only came into existence with the development of societies large enough that it was not possible for "everyone" to know "everyone else's" whereabouts and activities at all times. The earliest humans lived in very small communities. All members knew one another well and agreed automatically to live by the same set of rules, customs, and moral standards. To the extent that any one individual did deviate from such rules, customs, and moral standards, he or she

---

Tourists pose for pictures in the stocks at Colonial Williamsburg in Virginia. In the past, informal social controls such as ostracism, and public punishments such as the stocks, effectively curtailed criminal behavior. Today society relies on a large, well-organized police force.

Regulators lynch a black man. The Regulators, a vigilante group, were considered a huge success at first; later they were seen as out-of-control extremists. Their arbitrary violence alienated so-called respectable people, and the Regulators fell out of favor.

might be sanctioned, punished, or brought back into line by any number of informal control methods—shunning or ostracizing the deviant person, shaming them through gossip, or administering more brutal physical or psychological punishments in the name of vengeance and justice.

Today, such informal methods of social control continue to exist in certain forms. The set of rules, rewards, and punishments imposed by parents constitutes a kind of informal control mechanism—one that will vary in terms of strictness, fairness, flexibility, consistency, and so on, from household to household. Another form of social control is the often cruel and arbitrary-seeming "system" of jokes, taunts, and humiliations that schoolchildren will use against peers who don't fit the group's accepted standards of appearance or behavior.

From the two foregoing examples, it should be clear that the mere existence of enforceable social standards does not automatically imply justice, fairness, compassion, equality, or any of the other positive values that democratic societies have claimed to care about. There is nothing obviously good or just about the conformity that schoolchildren impose upon each other. And while most parents, for example, have only the best intentions when they establish and enforce rules—they hope to help their children become responsible, moral, mature adults who can lead structured, productive lives—some parents, acting as the family "police" power, are capable of overzealous behavior, unfairness, arbitrariness, even bullying and brutality. (Even families, Skolnick might say, are subject to the law and order dilemma.)

Formal social control systems, such as the police and the entire criminal justice system of courts and prisons, are the institutions that have replaced informal methods in today's large human societies, where most people are strangers to one another and cannot effectively police themselves. An interesting case from the 18th century illustrates the way such institutions can easily cross the line between supporting the common good and threatening it (in much the same way that parents can sometimes cross the line from reinforcing to destroying the health of the family).

In many rural backcountry areas of South Carolina during the Cherokee War of 1760–1761, landowning families had fled to the safety of forts. When the war was over and they returned, these people found their homelands overrun by opportunistic outlaw gangs, who robbed houses, killed or tortured the owners, raped women, stole horses and slaves, and abducted young girls. In the absence of any local law enforcement agency or court system, the citizens of the area banded together informally and began a series of counterattacks on the outlaw camps. Eventually this informal vigilante group, known as the Regulators, came to be recognized and reinforced by the state's governor and legislature back in the capital city of Charleston.

For a few years, the Regulators were considered a huge success, as they proved to be very effective in catching outlaws and retrieving abducted girls and stolen horses. They were the heroes of respectable society. But in 1768, with the outlaw problem under control, the Regulators started to view themselves as absolute moral arbiters and took it upon themselves to rid the backcountry of "lower people"—vagrants, idlers, sexually promiscuous women, and anyone else who didn't measure up to their bourgeois standards of respectability. In a sense, the Regulators' modus operandi might be seen as a precursor to the broken windows or zero tolerance approaches to policing that became popular again two and a half centuries later. By 1769, however, it became clear even to many of the so-called respectable people that the Regulators had gone too far in their campaign of arbitrary terror and punishment for what were, after all, fairly minor crimes. They had tipped the balance between law and order too far in the latter direction—and they had crossed the line from good cop to bad cop. The group was eventually stripped of its power and replaced by a newly established formal court system for the region.

Then and now, there is a continuous struggle for an equitable power distribution between ordinary citizens in need of protection and the agents chosen to protect them. But exactly who will do the policing? Under what specific circumstances or set of laws? And with what level of physical and legal power over other people? Since any given society is in a constant state of change, the answers to these questions are always shifting.

In early England, from which our own present-day system largely derives, local people were responsible for their own policing on a voluntary, nonprofessional basis. A few hundred years later, in the cramped, dirty, fortified cities of preindustrial England, citizens were still dependent on a voluntary surveillance system known as the night watch. All townspeople took turns

Early England relied on a night watch system for protection from crime. Citizens took turns participating in the night watch, but merchants and businessmen began paying people to take their places. This "Charley" is an early paid night watchman equipped with lantern, noisemaker, and stick.

policing the narrow alleys of the city, keeping an eye out for thieves, guarding the gates against intruders, sounding alarms in case of fire. As time went on and cities became larger, however, people grew tired of volunteering for the obligatory night watch job, since it took so much time away from their primary work. Merchants and businessmen began paying other people to take their place in the night watch. But these employers were looking for cheap labor, so the night watch employees generally came from the ranks of the old, poor, or lame—people ill-equipped to deal with the criminal element.

Eventually, someone hit upon the idea of offering financial incentives to attract a better class of night watchmen. In 1692, the English Parliament passed the

The Bow Street Runners were paid detectives who paved the way for an English police force. These Bow Street Runners are protecting King George III from an angry mob.

Highwayman Act, which provided rewards to anyone who captured a criminal. Thus was created a whole new class of businessman, the "thief taker" or bounty hunter. This was the beginning of a long, recurring history of reforms, innovations, and attempts to "professionalize" the police force. But the idea predictably backfired: these bounty hunters quickly figured out how to get rich easily by framing innocent people.

Crime was rampant in the cities of this era, despite the fact that many serious offenses carried the death penalty. Public hangings were a common spectacle. And yet prostitutes, pickpockets, and more brutal kinds of criminals virtually lined the streets. In response, England developed the Bow Street Runners, a group of paid detectives who traveled to major crime scenes, examined the evidence, and launched manhunts for the perpetrators. Their success in solving crimes led to increased public acceptance for the idea of an established, paid police force, and led the way to Parliament's Metropolitan Police Act of 1829. A thousand men were chosen to serve under the direction of Sir Robert Peel, who came to be known as the father of modern policing. Peel's "bobbies" (nicknamed after him) were uniformed but not armed, except for a short truncheon or baton they kept concealed under their coats. These uniformed officers were out and about in public view, and therefore served (at least in theory) as a deterrent to criminal activity.

In the political climate of today's United States, many people think of themselves as antigovernment. They claim to hate taxes and the Internal Revenue Service, or to mistrust international cooperative organizations such as the United Nations or the World Bank, or to feel that the federal legislature and executive offices in Washington, D.C., are filled with cowards, charlatans, and rogues. Vehement antigovernment sentiment has a long and venerable pedigree in this country, so it should come as no surprise that for many decades, U.S. citizens were largely reluctant to establish any kind of official, paid law enforcement agency. During the decades after the Revolutionary War, the sight of armed, uniformed, quasi-military governmental agents would have caused much distress for a generation of citizens who had just escaped the yoke of British occupation.

In the next century, while America's westward boundary pushed closer and closer to the Pacific Ocean, the notion of a standing police force would have run contrary to the frontiersmen's ideas of American freedom and liberty. Ultimately, this distaste for established law enforcement meant that the persons who ended up in charge of maintaining public order were volunteers or reluctant conscripts. In either case, they were definitely not trained professionals. For

In the frontier towns of the American West, the line between lawman and outlaw was often quite thin. Sometimes the only men willing to undertake the dangerous work of maintaining order had a propensity for deadly violence themselves.

example, in the early 19th century, in the patchily populated, unorganized western territories—the American frontier—the town sheriff or town marshal was often just a hair's breadth away from being a criminal himself. Frank Prassel described these men in his classic study from 1972, *The Western Peace Officer*:

Earp, Hickock, Masterson—such names are synonymous with the image of the western town marshal. Their legend is one of a tall lone figure, striding down a dusty street in the dim direction of public order and immortality. It is a myth, yet one based on a slim foundation of truth. . . .

What kinds of men filled these offices? In some villages they came from the ranks of local toughs, on the theory that such persons would most easily gain the fearful respect of the region's criminal element. Occasionally personnel of such dubious qualifications were the only volunteers willing to undertake the work. Unfortunate results, of course, often followed this method of selection. Some local marshals had to flee the community when made to appear cowardly; others resigned after disgraceful public performances caused by drink and gross abuses of office.

Until the 19th century, then, American law enforcement was mostly an ad hoc affair, handled idiosyncratically by each jurisdiction, and often driven by desperation rather than an attitude of calm civic planning. In the frontier lands, vigilantism was the primary form of social control. Groups of generally upstanding townspeople, often led by a prominent citizen such as a banker or doctor, would take matters into their own hands when outlaws threatened their lives and livelihoods. As with the South Carolina Regulators, there was always the potential for these groups to cross over the line from constructive to destructive actions. In many cases, it was only such regrettable situations that finally convinced people of the need for an official police force that could be held accountable for its actions.

Meanwhile, in the cities of this era, paid police forces were beginning to be organized in a more formal manner than on the frontier. In 1833, Philadelphia established a 24-man daytime police force to supplement its 120 night watchmen. Boston took similar action in 1838. By 1870, just about every major American city had a full-time police force. But these institutions still lacked any kind of training or any idea of professional standards. Despite some attempts in the 1880s and 1890s to create a physically and mentally fit police force through training programs, late-19th-century law enforcement agencies were rife with incompetence. The problem of poor training was exacerbated by the fact of widespread corruption and patronage, especially in large cities. A prime example was New York City's police department under the control of the notoriously corrupt Tammany Hall government. Appointments to police jobs and promotions within the department were normally dependent upon the payment of fees to Tammany politicians. Police officers in turn tried to recoup those fees by blackmailing brothel owners and saloon keepers. It was a kickback system as entrenched and ubiquitous as the one Frank Serpico would bring to light 100 years later in the same city, and it made common criminals out of the very people who'd sworn to fight crime.

Urban police work was low-paying, dangerous, and therefore attractive only to people who had few other options for livelihood. Furthermore, there was very little in the way of training or professional hiring standards for law enforcement officers—a problem that persisted until the mid-20th century. Officers sometimes received their jobs in exchange for political favors. Men with criminal records were hired as patrolmen. Many police officers were grammar-school dropouts. Even as late as the mid-1930s, an investigative survey found that nearly 200 American cities had placed new officers on the streets without any training, without providing partners, and without asking if the rookies knew how to shoot the service revolver they'd been issued.

Law enforcement in the South had a distinct history of its own, in that southern policing generally grew out of the old slave patrols—America's first homegrown police system that was not borrowed from English models. Here we have a clear historical example of the way a formal social control mechanism could be put in the service of values and priorities that later generations have come to judge as wrong or even evil. By the standards of their own time and place, the slave patrols of the colonial era were simply doing their job as well as possible: they policed specific geographic beats and were authorized to stop, search, whip, or even kill African slaves for infractions against local law, for being off their plantations after curfew or without their owner's permission, for trying to run away, or for attempting to organize slave rebellions. By today's standards, slave patrols were simply the brutal tools of a system of racial oppression and economic exploitation.

Extrapolating from the past, one realizes that today's current standards of police practice will also be judged by future generations. Which practices will come to be viewed as barbaric, or as the product of a fundamentally unjust social system, the way we now generally view the practices of the slave patrols? Which innovations in police administration will seem as farsighted and effective as Sir Robert Peel's bobbies? Which local agencies will be accused—as the Regulators eventually were— of crossing the line from heroes to villains?

In the aftermath of the Civil War and particularly in the first two decades of the 20th century before World War I, a growing reform movement focused on efforts to combat rampant corruption, inefficiency, and injustice in many spheres of public life—including legislatures, city halls, and police stations. This was the era that ushered in several features of modern life that we now take for granted, such as women's right to vote and hold public office, and labor protection laws to limit the maximum number of work hours per day and week. The Progressive Movement, as it came to be known, also

Sir Robert Peel became the father of modern policing. His 1,000 uniformed "bobbies" (nicknamed for him) were not armed, except for a short baton. They were out and about in public view and served as a deterrent to criminal activity. The bobby has become one of the distinctive sights of London.

instituted merit-based systems for hiring and promoting police officers, thereby eliminating or at least threatening the kickback culture of the era.

The burgeoning police professionalization movement picked up steam even while other progressive efforts lost ground during the troubled years between World War I and the Great Depression. America was becoming a more urban country. By 1929, its cities contained 56 percent of the entire U.S. population, compared with 40 percent in 1900. So urban police chiefs, in particular, were concerned with bringing structure and efficiency to their agencies. Comparative studies between U.S. and European police departments strongly suggested the need for officers who were both better educated in general and well trained for the specific requirements of police work. In the 1920s, J. Edgar Hoover put such suggestions into action as he transformed the Federal Bureau of Investigation into a highly trained and structured investigative force. Probably the most influential reformer of the era was August Vollmer, chief of police in Berkeley, California. His stringent standards for the education, professional conduct, and even personal moral conduct of police officers continue to influence the way present-day law enforcement agencies perceive their role in society. He was perhaps the first person to articulate a coherent vision of the good cop.

In a 1919 article entitled "The Policeman as a Social Worker," Vollmer argued that police officers—"our peace guardians," as he called them—had "far more important and far greater obligations than the mere apprehending and prosecuting of lawbreakers." Vollmer urged the police to join efforts with schools, churches, recreation and juvenile departments, hospitals, public welfare agencies, employment bureaus, and all other interested community partners in trying to address the root causes of criminal behavior. His perspective echoed many Progressive Era values: Vollmer believed, for example, that most criminals behaved badly out of economic desperation or because they lacked strong moral training in childhood.

In retrospect, this vision of the police officer's all-healing moral power seems a bit naive, perhaps even condescending. For example, Vollmer wrote, "Wayward girls may be saved from taking the final plunge into a life of evil, and many homes saved from disgrace and sadness, by the kindly counsel of the policeman. Sick and poor [who might otherwise turn to theft] may be directed to the established places for their relief. These cases should be carefully followed up and nothing left undone which would be of assistance in their rehabilitation." Vollmer may have been oversimplifying the origins of crime and also expecting far too much from police officers. Yet his notion that the law enforcement official should play an integral role in the larger community—along with the idea that police officers need to cultivate the skills of social workers—would be echoed 60 years later by a new generation of reformers and by advocates of community policing.

Vollmer's direct protégé was a man named O. W. (Orlando Winfield) Wilson, whose 1950 textbook, *Police Administration*, was considered the bible for U.S. police chiefs through the next two or three decades. In the

Police chief August Vollmer of Berkeley, California, was one of the first to set standards for the education, professional conduct, and moral conduct of police officers. He urged police officers to join with the community to address root causes of crime.

book, Wilson advocated a quasi-military hierarchy within police agencies and emphasized police training and integrity. He also articulated the many factors transforming police work in that area: rapid urban population increases; the ubiquity of automobiles and their use by criminals; and increased traffic accidents and congestion, the handling of which represented a larger and larger proportion of the police officer's workload. While incorporating new challenges, Wilson remained true to his mentor's central vision, articulating a positive—and profoundly optimistic— "philosophy of service" for police officers:

> The old police philosophy of "throw 'em in jail" has changed to a new philosophy of keeping people out of jail. . . . Police service today extends beyond mere routine investigation and disposition of complaints; it also has as its objective the welfare of the individual and of society. If society is to be effectively safeguarded against crime, the police must actively seek out and destroy delinquency-inducing influences in the community and assist in providing suitable treatment for the maladjusted.

Despite its strong advocates, such as Wilson, this progressive, socially inclined notion of police was fundamentally at odds with another, more antagonistic style of law enforcement—a style that reemerged later in the zero-tolerance attitudes adopted in the 1990s in New York City and elsewhere. William H. Parker, who was head of the Los Angeles Police Department from 1950 to 1966 (and who, incidentally, served as a consultant to the popular television series *Dragnet*), was perhaps the first to use the words "war on crime" as a central battle cry for his officers. Although Parker and Wilson were mutually supportive of each other's approaches, it eventually became clear that, as one history book puts it, "Parker's focus on the 'war on crime' often prevented him from paying adequate attention to other important concerns such as race relations—a mistake the LAPD continued to make well into the 1990s." Still, Parker was as instrumental as his forebears in pushing the police toward a more professional model of behavior through discipline, efficiency, and very high recruitment standards.

Parker knew his history. He once wrote that the story of policing in the United States was "one of alternating inefficiency, corruption, and brutality." For this reason, he understood why there was so little cooperation, trust, or support from the public for law enforcement activities. But he remained an optimist about the future. In 1954 he wrote, "The last few years have seen a great upsurge of attention to this aspect of government [i.e., the police] and, even more heartening, a growing appreciation of the vital part [law enforcement] plays in the affairs of men. If this rising tide of interest can be sustained, the professional police services our country so critically needs may, within our lifetime, be planned and their foundations laid."

Were Parker alive today, he would probably be quite pleased with the relatively high level of professional standards upheld, at least in theory, by most major police forces across this nation. At the same time, he would have to note that problems with corruption and brutality persist. "Professionalism," while certainly improving upon the random, unregulated vigilantism of the past, cannot entirely erase the good cop/bad cop tension inherent in the enterprise.

3

THE WHO
AND WHY OF
POLICE WORK

The long, dark, complex history of policing reveals it to be an institution that generates villainy as often as heroism—maybe more often. While the structure and function of policing in a democratic society is itself a source of conflict and problems (as Skolnick and others have documented), the kind of individuals involved in police work certainly play a role in the overall good and bad behavior of the institution.

Early-20th-century reformers had a fairly idealized view of the police officers of the future. As one historian puts it, men like August Vollmer envisioned "highly trained and well-rounded college men who approached their jobs with gentlemanly demeanor and knightly virtue." Vollmer once noted that citizens expected police officers "to have the wisdom of Solomon, the courage of David, the strength of Samson, the patience of Job, the leadership of Moses, the kindness of the Good Samaritan, the strategical [*sic*] training

nbers of the Cadet Class No. 77 of Kentucky State Police Academy • for a graduation photo. Police rtments across the United States seeking greater racial, ethnic, and ler diversity among their recruits.

45

of Alexander, the faith of Daniel, the diplomacy of Lincoln, the tolerance of the Carpenter of Nazareth, and, finally, an intimate knowledge of every branch of the natural, biological, and social sciences. If he had all these, he *might* be a good policeman."

The reality of the time was that most policemen were "grossly underpaid, poorly trained, and undereducated," and "their social peers were laborers who built and maintained the cities and the cars that began to crowd their streets, not the lawyers, accountants, bankers, and merchants who sat in offices."

Today, despite the existence of college-level law enforcement curricula and, in some cases, entire institutions devoted to criminology, police work remains a primarily blue-collar occupation. It wasn't until very recently that college-educated police officers became common, and they are generally still not the majority in most police agencies. Fifty or 60 years ago, police work offered upward mobility to many people who had few other options to escape the lower-class or lower-middle-class life from which they came. Many men who served in the military during World War II came home to become police officers—a good fit in most cases, because these men already understood the use of firearms, the meaning of putting one's life at risk on behalf of others, and the nature of hierarchical command structures. In some cases, veterans received bonus points in applications for law enforcement jobs.

The social upheavals of the civil rights era left a mark upon law enforcement as much as any other public institution. As a result, a police force that was almost all-white, almost all-male, almost all high school educated at best, and predominantly military in cultural orientation is slowly being replaced by a force that includes women, racial minorities, college graduates, and (to some undetermined extent) out-of-the-closet gays and lesbians.

American women first entered policing in the 1830s, in the special, limited role of police matrons, whose only obligation was to oversee women inmates in local prisons—a job that, by the standards of the time, was considered both too delicate and too unimportant for male police officers to handle. The nascent women's rights movement helped push for new policies regarding women police in the early 20th century, although it wasn't until the 1960s that women began working routine patrol duty. As late as 1981, only 5.5 percent of all sworn police officers were women.

The history of black police in America is intimately and paradoxically bound up with the history of slavery and racial oppression. African slaves in America were a troublesome presence, as one historian, W. Marvin Dulaney, has written. "Belying their captors' claim that they were made for slavery, Africans rebelled against the institution in a variety of ways"—refusing to work, destroying crops and farm implements, killing livestock, poisoning their owners, and sometimes running away or organizing rebellions. By the start of the 18th century, most American colonies had established special law codes for slaves and special slave patrol units. In the South throughout the 18th and 19th centuries, the ranks of these paramilitary slave patrols were usually filled with poor white men—another example of the era's reliance on relatively desperate people to do the community's "dirty work." After the Civil War and the abolition of slavery, black police officers were

The first policewomen were given duties of little or no importance. Here a 1920s' policewoman enforces Chicago's swimsuit laws.

Before the Civil War, the South organized slave patrol units. These paramilitary patrols were filled with poor white men—an example of the era's reliance on desperate people to do the community's "dirty work."

still extremely rare and most often hired to patrol "their own kind" in all-black ghettoes and neighborhoods. They were usually prohibited by law and custom from arresting a white person. It wasn't until the late 1960s and 1970s that blacks were represented in any significant numbers on major metropolitan police forces as full-fledged officers of the law.

As America becomes a more diverse place, so does the police force—especially in urban areas. In 1988, a writer named Harvey Rachlin spent a year following one class of recruits at the New York Police Academy for his 1991 book *The Making of a Cop*. The 650 recruits in this particular class were, Rachlin said, a typically heterogeneous group that mirrored "the melting pot it will protect. There are whites and blacks. Irish, Italians, Hispanics, Orientals, Germans, Jamaicans, and Poles. Catholics, Protestants, and Jews. The recruits are youthful and robust men and women, ranging in size from towering to petite."

But the increasing presence of women, blacks, and other "nontraditional" police officers raises a number of questions that have yet to be answered—mostly because this development is still rather new and can't be observed with enough historical distance. The primary question is whether a more-diverse, better-educated force will harbor fewer bad cops. It is a hopeful notion, but those who view policing as an inherently problematic institution would probably look upon it skeptically. And the record thus far backs up the skeptics, to some extent. During the 1940s and 1950s, for example, when black officers were expected under segregation to police black citizens, these men often overcompensated with zealous and brutal enforcement habits in order to prove they were real cops. Their presence as representatives of their race did not necessarily make life any easier for the citizens over whom they had power.

In the not-too-distant past, as we've seen, the people charged with maintaining public order were often just a hair's breadth away—in terms of social class, education, or proclivity for violence—from the ruffians and criminals they sought to arrest. A person's motivation for becoming a police officer was all too often the simple fact that he (almost never *she*) had no other prospects in life. Times have changed, for the most part. Unlike their counterparts from centuries or even decades in the past, today's police recruits are generally not motivated by the same kind of economic desperation and social pressures that helped fill the ranks of slave patrols or night watches. But now that police work is a bona fide profession, what kind of person decides to become a police officer? And what reasons motivate them to choose this unusually dangerous career path?

Many young people are drawn to police work through Hollywood. Shows like NYPD Blue *depict policing as a fast-paced, glamorous occupation. The reality of police work is often much different.*

For better or worse, plenty of young people are drawn to police work through Hollywood. Television shows and films tend to portray law enforcement as an exciting, fast-paced, challenging endeavor through which good consistently conquers evil. Recruits often allude to the police "mystique," the sense of coolness, unflappability, and palpable authority they've observed in cops. They are drawn, quite simply, to the power.

But successful police rookies soon learn that a good deal of the job involves drudgery, paperwork, and less-than-glamorous tasks such as writing traffic tickets. Furthermore, while the cop's primary responsibilities still have to do with law enforcement and the maintenance of public order, he or she is also charged to handle a broad range of service-related duties, such as managing the scene of a traffic accident—no matter how minor—or assisting a lost or injured person. To stick with the program, a police officer must be able to draw on a deeper and more realistic source of motivation than the easily debunked Hollywood image.

Some aspiring officers are driven simply by the idea of using their badge and their uniform to help other people. As one 1992 introductory textbook on law enforcement explains:

> Recent studies of why people become police officers uncover a distinct motivational shift. While salary and job security still merit some mention, a growing faction lists more altruistic reasons for entering the police world. The opportunity to help other less fortunate people and to improve society has become a magnet. This social service theme is a radical departure from traditional law and order concerns. At least one researcher argues that we are witnessing the induction of a new breed of police officers.

Stuart Gellman's 1993 book, *Cops: The Men and Women Behind the Badge*, illustrates some of the reasons why people decide to become cops, as well as the various types of backgrounds police officers come from. Gellman followed one class of Arizona police recruits through the hiring, academy training, and field training process. Pat Batelli, a woman who formerly worked as a nurse, had dreamed of a police career since childhood. Her grandfather had been a beloved and respected neighborhood cop in Paterson, New Jersey, and decades later she still thought back proudly upon the deep compassion and caring he exemplified in his work every day. Another recruit was Les Beach, a 45-year-old navy

Police officers train for many types of situations. These Hong Kong riot police officers are training for special tactics involving a helicopter.

veteran when he moved to Tucson specifically to join the force; he'd also wanted to be a cop since childhood, but 20 years earlier he had failed a physical to become a New York State Trooper. He had flat feet—a pointless disqualification that dated back to the era when troopers rode horses, but one that had not yet been lifted off the law books. A third recruit was Rene Gomez, a native Tucsonian who'd been pursuing a college degree in art and working in his mother's Mexican restaurant. Many of the restaurant patrons were police officers, who'd tell stories of their daily experiences with the particular blend of cynicism and gallows humor that cops are known for. Rene was fascinated enough to start envisioning this life for himself.

For many people, pursuing a life in law enforcement entails a great deal of personal risk and challenge. Derek Campbell, a Tucson recruit who had previously worked as a cop in Chicago, had actually lost his marriage over his job. He'd spent three months at the police academy there, and then two days after he was assigned to the streets, his wife told him she didn't want to be married to a cop. Although it meant an unwanted divorce, he was not ready to change his mind about his calling. Anita Sueme, a college graduate with a degree in microbiology, had to overcome a good deal of personal insecurity to make her way into the company of Tucson's police recruits. A shy person by nature, she had spent five years as a police radio dispatcher, telling the mostly male officers where to go and what to do. Although this position naturally boosted her assertiveness and self-confidence, she still failed the psychological examination portion of the police application and was told that her personality was too passive. Ironically, this rejection actually spurred her to become more determined and assertive. She tried again a second time, and was accepted. The process had taught her exactly how stubborn she could be.

Police hiring and education is a far more serious business now than it was 100 years ago. Up until the 1920s, police officers didn't even receive regular training in firearms, although in many jurisdictions cops had been walking around with service revolvers since the middle of the 19th century. The efforts of early-20th-century reformers to achieve a more professional and effective police force eventually led to the kind of rigorous, intensive police academy programs used throughout the United States today.

Considering the fact that many early Americans bristled at the idea of an official quasi-military force policing their streets and curtailing their hard-won

The police academy is very much like an army boot camp. Instructors bark orders and expect cadets to work to their physical and mental limit. These Virginia State Police cadets stand at attention while an instructor checks regulation bed making with a ruler.

freedom, it is ironic that modern police training has indeed borrowed a lot of its methods and attitudes from military culture. When writer Stuart Gellman followed Pat Batelli, Rene Gomez, Derek Campbell, and a number of other Tucson City Police Department recruits to their first day at Arizona's police academy, they were greeted by a foulmouthed, browbeating senior officer who sneered, "You're in for eleven weeks of hell. You don't f—ing impress me so far; you look like a d—n bunch of misfits." The recruits—or cadets, as they were called—would have to meet fairly tough academic and physical performance standards during their time in the academy. Major examinations would be held every Friday, and any score below 75 percent would be considered a failing grade. Two failed exams meant immediate dismissal. Physical standards varied with the age of the cadet, but women and men would have to meet the same standards. For example, a 26-year-old police cadet would meet the minimum requirement by doing 24 push-ups and 39 sit-ups a minute, jumping 19 inches vertically from a standing position, completing the agility sprint in 18 seconds, and running 1.5 miles in 13 minutes. In addition to the academic and physical training, there would be 40 hours of firearms instruction, as well as instruction in first aid, search techniques, felony stops, and defensive driving. In any of these areas, failure to meet performance guidelines would result in dismissal. Gellman wrote:

> "You won't all make it through," Tucson Police Department Lieutenant Tom Patterson tells the group two weeks before they enter the Academy. "Some of you will drop out and others will be asked to leave. You're going to a strict and rigid environment where your decisions will be made for you. They'll yell at you and scream at you and you're not going to like it. They'll try to stress you out physically and mentally, because if you can't take it there, you won't be able to take it on the street where some people will try to hurt you. You're not a failure if you change your mind. If this is absolutely, positively what you want to do in life, you'll probably make it. If you've made a mistake, you'll know it soon."

For all that, Arizona's "eleven weeks of hell" was still not necessarily the most rigorous or demanding program available in the late 1980s and early 1990s. The police recruits in Rachlin's book, *The Making of a Cop,* were obliged to complete an intense six-month program at the police academy before being assigned to a precinct for six additional months of field training. For five days a week, eight hours a day, recruits attended classes covering everything from the mechanics of ticket-writing to the ever-changing minutiae of state criminal law. They then spent all weekend and

Marksmanship is among the many skills a recruit must master to graduate from the police academy.

every evening preparing their homework for these subjects. They sweated and panted their way through grueling gym sessions—running laps, learning boxing punches and self-defense moves, working their bodies to achieve peak physical conditioning. They took classes in social science, which challenged them to put aside their personal prejudices in working with other people, emphasized the use of strong listening and observation skills, instructed them in ways to analyze people's behavior and judge situations accurately, and taught them how to defuse rather than escalate arguments with members of the public. They listened with a heady combination of awe, fear, and envy as their instructors—veteran street cops, for the most part—told gripping tales about their own struggles with dangerous suspects or their close brushes with death by whizzing machine-gun fire. They went through thorough firearms training and took a driving course. They acted out dozens of dangerous scenarios in which they often were "killed" by criminals they were pursuing.

Stringent rules and regulations governed these recruits, both at the academy and in their off-duty hours. Technically, the students were already "probationary" police officers—they were, of course, already drawing a salary—but they would not receive their guns and "shields" (badges) until they graduated from the academy. Until the 1970s, Rachlin noted, the department issued guns and shields to recruits just a few days into the academy. "Background investigations were not extensive then, and those at the academy old enough to remember report wild episodes: students frisking one another in the halls with their weapons drawn, revolvers being cocked in bathroom stalls. A couple of recruits even held up a bank." In another incident around 1960, a recruit shot and killed a teenager who'd been causing some minor mischief in the neighborhood.

Although the recruits were dressed in uniform each day, they were not expected to respond to crimes yet. At the same time, they were already sworn officers of the court, having taken an oath to uphold the laws of the state upon entering the academy. So any illegal behavior—staying at a bar past the city's legal closing time of 4 A.M., for example, or getting into a brawl— would result in immediate dismissal.

The quasi-military culture of the academy revealed itself most clearly in PT, physical training. It was here that some instructors would don the persona of a screaming drill sergeant: standing over recruits, "haranguing them to snap to attention quickly, not to slack off during exercises, to squeeze out that last ounce of energy in the thirty-sixth lap." Much attention was paid to self-defense

The officers involved in the Amadou Diallo shooting were white and their victim was black. This exacerbated tensions and renewed questions about racism in law enforcement. In response, the New York City Police Department instituted sensitivity training to help defuse the tense relationship between police and the minority community.

techniques: breaking falls; tackling suspects; getting free from choke holds, headlocks, or bear hugs; resisting knife attacks. PT was also the place where recruits first learned the most effective and legally proper techniques for frisking and handcuffing suspects—tasks that required a surprising amount of attention to detail. Rachlin described this training in *The Making of a Cop:*

Officer Dave Washington demonstrates the process for Company 20. Approaching the perp (played by a student officer) from behind at a distance of six to eight feet, the officer makes strong eye contact with the suspect, and in a loud, authoritative voice shouts, "Police! Don't move!" He orders the suspect to turn around or go up against the wall. Then, if the officer is right-handed, he takes two steps to his left, because if the suspect suddenly turns around with a gun, he will probably shoot where he heard the voice coming from. If the officer is left-handed, he takes two steps to the right. A right-handed officer will frisk the left side first. Then come the orders:

"Put your hands straight up."
"Wiggle your fingers." Dirt, razor blades, or any other object he may be concealing between his fingers fall free.
"Face your palms toward me.
"Turn your head to the right.
"Spread your legs wide.
"Bring your feet back toward me." The point is to keep the perp off balance if he is against the wall.

As the representative police academies of New York and Arizona demonstrate, the intentions of early-20th-century reformers in the police professionalization movement have been realized to a great degree. But because there is, and presumably always will be, an ongoing struggle to define the proper scope and limits of police actions and police power, many people continue to question whether law enforcement officers are receiving enough training, and enough of the right *kind* of training.

Consider the situation of New York City's police department in the aftermath of the Amadou Diallo shooting. As noted earlier, the officers involved were white, while the victim was black, a fact that exacerbated an already tense relationship between the police department and the city's minority communities and that reengaged long-standing questions regarding racism in law enforcement.

The NYPD responded to charges of racism by beefing up its focus on "sensitivity" and "diversity" training at the academy. But not all observers felt this to be a sensible response. In late 2000, a conservative think tank called The Manhattan Institute published an article by writer Heather MacDonald in its quarterly publication, *City Journal*. MacDonald, who spent time observing the academy's training program, wrote very skeptically—indeed, dismissively—about the NYPD's renewed focus on combating racism at the recruit level. Anyone who has ever actually set foot inside the police academy, MacDonald wrote, "would have to conclude that the NYPD has forged a training message as relentlessly focused on restraint and respect as anyone could hope for." Rather than focusing on what she called "moronic" discussions regarding race, diversity, and sensitivity, the academy should be "teaching officers to respond appropriately to challenges to their authority."

MacDonald also argued against the mainstream interpretation of what had happened to Diallo. In her view, race had nothing to do with why this innocent man was shot to death in the doorway of his own apartment building. The situation arose out of bad tactics, plain and simple.

> The NYPD's tactical mantra is "cover, concealment, and communication." The first two imperatives buy an officer time and protection to figure out the nature of the threat and the safest way of defusing it. The third imperative means: communicate with fellow officers, the suspect, and civilians. Failure of all three C's resulted in the death of Amadou Diallo. The four street-crime officers too quickly left the cover of their cars to approach Diallo's apartment vestibule; they had no apparent plan of action. Once they believed he was pointing a gun at them, they were fully exposed and had no recourse but to "shoot back," as they mistakenly, tragically, believed they were doing.

MacDonald went even further to say that the 1997 brutalization of Abner Louima was not primarily a racial bias case. "Rather than race, the Louima case was about something far more difficult to solve: officers [such as Justin Volpe] who treat resistance [from someone they're trying to arrest] as a personal affront." The only solution—albeit an imperfect one—would be for the NYPD to continue stressing courtesy, restraint, and nonphysical methods of generating voluntary compliance, such as " 'verbal judo,' a set of verbal steps for talking people into compliance."

In completely discounting the complicated interplay between race and power in law enforcement, as well as the centuries-long record of antagonism between the police and minority communities, MacDonald could reasonably be accused of simplifying matters and ignoring history. But her perspective echoes the long line of law enforcement reformers who have touted "professionalism" and thorough training as the only way—albeit, an imperfect way—to address some of the institution's problems.

Reality Meets the Badge

Plenty of rookies drop out when they realize that police work is not always the exciting, challenging, heroic venture they'd dreamed of as children. There's a lot of paperwork, a lot of time put into appearing in court to testify against suspects, a lot of effort put into relatively minor calls—cats caught in trees, keys locked in vehicles, complaints about noisy Saturday night parties, loud, belligerent arguments in bars that stop just short of violence. Yet the possibility of real danger lurks in each and every shift. During an eight-hour shift an officer can veer wildly from boredom to adrenaline-pumping fear, from writing up a dozen routine speeding tickets to pursuing a machine-gun-toting drug smuggler in a high-speed car chase.

Rookies who make it through training and stick with the job for more than a few months are on the path to becoming that very special breed of animal: the experienced street cop. Police officers who have worked for just a few years, particularly in large cities, eventually come to see a broader, uglier, more bizarre range of human behavior and experience than most ordinary civilians will witness in their entire lifetime. This creates a bond among police officers, but it also opens up a kind of social and emotional chasm between the police and other people. Even the most verbal and articulate police officers have trouble explaining to civilians all the crazy things they see and learn in the course of each shift. Feeling misunderstood by their noncop friends and loved ones, feeling misrepresented by TV, movie, and newspaper accounts, they may love to trade stories among themselves but tend to clam up around outsiders.

Ultimately, though, MacDonald admitted that training is not a panacea. "Reality . . . is the biggest challenge for the police," she asserted. "The enthusiasm with which most recruits begin their training wanes after only a few years on the streets. Police are lied to, betrayed, and cursed at by the people they are trying to help; they see communities close ranks around criminals; they are called into scenes of utter depravity."

As NYPD academy director James O'Keefe told MacDonald, "There is a very complex erosion of the human spirit that goes on in policing. Good people are exposed to bad things constantly. Officers start to ask whether the job is even doable." In such an environment, it is perhaps no surprise that situations like the Louima and Diallo cases do occasionally take place, despite all the efforts put into training and professionalism. Perhaps what's really surprising is that these extreme cases don't take place more often.

In 1990, in *Police: The Law Officer's Magazine*, a writer named Ed Nowicki raised the following challenge to American law enforcement training standards as they currently exist:

> Our great nation's police officers receive an average of 400 hours of training to make split-second decisions, while Justices of the Supreme Court may take months to review the correctness of those same decisions.
>
> I find it difficult to believe that to bury the dead [i.e., to become a licensed mortician], a person must have 60 college credits, 1 year apprenticeship, and 9 months of mortuary school. If you make a mistake, it's for darn sure the person being buried won't complain. Yet to be a law enforcement officer, charged with the responsibility of keeping people safe and alive, 400 hours is considered sufficient.
>
> Is it me, or are society's priorities out of order?

Nowicki's point sounds inarguable, and yet there are those officers who do argue against it—who believe 400 hours of training is already too much. For some veterans, the things they learned at the academy were so theoretical as to be almost useless in actual practice. Ultimately, they might say, the only credential that counts is your "street degree"—the practical knowledge you build, each and every shift, through intimate encounters with crime, criminals, and the more extreme aspects of human nature.

LAW VERSUS ORDER

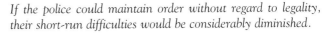

*If the police could maintain order without regard to legality,
their short-run difficulties would be considerably diminished.*

> —from *Justice Without Trial* by Jerome
> Skolnick (1966)

Two and a half centuries ago, vigilante groups like the South Carolina Regulators—self-appointed keepers of social order, who defined the crimes, captured the offenders, and dispensed the punishments as they saw fit—came into existence in rural and remote places precisely because there was no larger judicial infrastructure in place. Civilians felt the dire need to take matters into their own hands, or to coerce or hire representatives to do so, whenever members of their

---

*These guards at Angola State Prison in Louisiana are one part of the
vast and complex American justice system. Police, the gatekeepers to
the entire system, play an especially visible and crucial role in the
functioning of justice.*

communities or outsiders broke the rules. Today, the American justice system is a vast and complex one covering all citizens in all geographic regions, even the most rural or remote, to some greater or lesser extent. The modern police officer is a gatekeeper to this larger system, which encompasses jails, courts, prisons, juvenile detention centers, and psychiatric facilities for the criminally insane, and which enlists the work of many judges, juries, prosecutors, defense attorneys, social workers, psychiatrists, corrections officers, and—in some states—executioners.

On a personal level, this gatekeeper role can be a source of pride and power for police officers when they witness justice being served, or a source of cynicism, moral outrage, and feelings of impotence when the system fails to punish criminals who deserve some retribution. On an institutional or social level, we can see how

Life on the Beat, Part 2

In late April 2000, the literary cop we've come to know as Russell—a very responsible and cautious young officer, it would seem from the evidence—came close to serious trouble when he let down his guard. It was a slow night, so Russell was patrolling the area "looking for someone doing something wrong." He saw a vehicle coming in his direction with one headlight out, so he decided to make a traffic stop. Many otherwise law-abiding citizens feel that traffic tickets are an annoyance and a waste of time when police officers should be out chasing "real criminals." But the fact is, the police uncover a surprisingly large amount of criminal activity—from drug smuggling to car theft to murder—in the course of stopping people for speeding or running stop signs.

"When the driver pulled over, he went up onto the sidewalk and back onto the roadway." As Russell suspected, the man was extremely drunk. "He failed all of the field sobriety tests badly. It was classic. When I placed him in handcuffs and walked him to the rear of my patrol car he became beligerant [*sic*]. Initially he refused to get into my car, but I talked him into it."

Russell then noticed that his backup officer—a sergeant, much more experienced than Russell—was giving him a disappointed look.

He said did you see that rifle on the back seat? Sure enough there was the back end of a rifle sticking up through some clothing. It looked so obvious now, I was not sure how I missed it. My heart sunk. I tried to think of all the this gatekeeper role leads directly to the so-called law and order dilemma. The police, after all, are merely working in the service of a higher authority, namely, the law. They are not the ultimate authority in and of themselves—in the common phrase, they are not "above the law" just because they are tasked with enforcing it. The police are "inevitably concerned with interpreting legality because of their use of *law* as an instrument of order," sociologist Jerome Skolnick has written. The substantive part of criminal law contains society's agreed-upon rules for the maintenance of social order. These rules define certain activities as crimes, put regulations in place to prohibit such activities, and set standards and principles for the investigation, arrest, and punishment of persons who engage in such activities. But another important part of criminal law is concerned with regulating the behavior of all the

times he could have shot me. I thought of all my mistakes. It made me sick. I always try to be so cautious. I try so hard to see all of the little details that make me a better officer. I felt as though I failed in a big way.

As if the missed rifle wasn't bad enough, Russell was in for another shock. He transported the drunk driver to jail and then went to talk to the sergeant.

He still had that concerned look on his face and I could hear it in his voice also. What he told me next shocked me even more. He said, come look at what I found just behind the drivers [*sic*] seat. It was a FULLY loaded revolver. I did not say much. I felt stupid. I also felt lucky. The Sgt. did not have to chew me out.

Russell was in for a long night of soul-searching. As it turned out, the man he arrested was very belligerent at the station house. "I realized that not only did he have the means to do harm to an officer, he had the personality to back those guns up."

Russell had allowed himself to believe that he was dealing with nothing more than a simple drunk. He was not keeping his mind open to all the possible dangers and pitfalls. "I am very happy that I can take the time to think about what I did wrong to prevent anything like that from ever happening again," he reports.

In earlier eras of American law enforcement, there were few legal restraints on the way police officers operated. Beginning in the 1920s the U.S. Supreme Court began to constrain the behavior of overzealous police officers, a process that continues to this day.

officials—cops, judges, lawyers, and so on—whose collective job it is to deal with citizens suspected, accused, or found guilty of crimes. What constitutes a legal search? What is a legal arrest? What kind of proof or evidence is needed to satisfactorily prosecute a suspect? Must an accused person be represented by a lawyer, and must that lawyer be deemed competent? Is the accused entitled to a fair trial? If so, what features define a trial as fair or not? These kinds of questions are continually being raised, answered, challenged, and answered again through our courts and legislative system.

This regulatory part of the law is largely concerned with the rights and liberties of individual citizens who've been accused of crimes. In a democracy, accused suspects and even convicted criminals retain certain rights protecting their privacy, their property, their freedom from undue physical harm, and so on. The need to protect these rights sometimes gets in the way of a cop's mission to bring criminals to justice. These rights therefore limit the ability of the police, as an institution, to impose order upon society. As Skolnick puts it,

> [T]he common juxtaposition of "law and order" is an oversimplification. Law is not merely an instrument of order, but may frequently be its adversary. There are communities that appear disorderly to some (such as bohemian communities valuing diversity), but which nevertheless maintain a substantial degree of legality. The contrary may also be found: a situation where order is well maintained, but where the policy and practice of legality is not evident. The totalitarian social system, whether in a nation or an institution, is a situation of order without rule of law.

In earlier eras of American law enforcement, there were few legal restraints on the way police officers operated. There were no guidelines or restrictions on searches of homes, cars, or persons or on seizures of private property. Beginning in the 1920s and 1930s and continuing through the 1960s, the U.S. Supreme Court began constraining the behavior of police officers by ruling that evidence obtained in violation of the Constitution—specifically, in violation of the Fourth Amendment's guarantee against unreasonable searches and seizures—would not be admissible in court. The Supreme Court decisions that pertain to this aspect of police work are still being refined today through new interpretations and rulings. But even at the time of one of the earliest cases, it was clearly difficult to strike a balance between the Fourth Amendment guarantee and the practical need for intrusive investigations. During Prohibition, for example, investigations of liquor bootleggers often required that the police dig into the personal lives of people who had no specific complaints or charges lodged against them. Similar conflicts arise today in contemporary drug law enforcement.

The nation's highest court also eventually articulated rules and principles governing the treatment of

THE YOKE.

THE PULLEYS.

BUCKING.

THE CROWN.

INTERIOR OF A CONVICT'S CELL.

EXTERIOR OF A CONVICT'S CELL.

Until the 20th century, crime suspects were subject to tortures of many types, and police frequently extracted confessions from the innocent as well as the guilty. This illustration depicts various tortures used in 19th-century law enforcement.

arrested suspects, often in response to governmental commissions documenting brutal practices. In his textbook *Introduction to Law Enforcement: An Insider's View*, William G. Doerner puts it this way:

> Not so long ago, the police did whatever they pleased with arrested persons. As a matter of fact, the record shows that the police often beat suspects unmercifully. Other times, they denied arrestees food and contact with family members. Sometimes the atrocities were reminiscent of how the enemy treated prisoners of war. As a result, even law-abiding and upstanding citizens grew fearful of their own police offers.

"The quest for truth in the determination of wrongdoing is replete with a variety of sordid practices," Doerner writes. During the European Middle Ages, suspects were generally considered guilty until proven innocent, and innocence could only be proven through a "trial by ordeal"—essentially, a torture session limited only by the perverse and illogical imaginations of the interrogators. "A person accused of a crime might put an arm in a vat of boiling water. If he or she emerged unscathed, that person was innocent. Some walked barefoot over a bed of hot embers and coals. Other tests called for the accused to handle a burning object or to jump into a river or pond with a heavy millstone tied around the neck."

Although the American legal system was founded upon the enlightened notion of "innocent until proven guilty," some early police methods exhibited a strong resemblance to their brutal antecedents. Up until the reforms of the early 20th century, police suspects were routinely whipped, starved, and beaten until their wills gave out and they offered up full confessions, even to crimes they had not committed. In the late 19th century, suspects were often subject to the "sweat box," a small room situated next to a large iron stove. A historian in 1910 described the process in a florid but probably accurate manner, as follows:

The legal appeal of convicted rapist and kidnapper Ernesto Miranda (right) led to the landmark 1966 Supreme Court decision in Miranda v. Arizona, *which requires police to inform suspects of certain rights upon arrest.*

The subject [i.e., suspect] indisposed to disclose information which might be securely locked within his bosom, without ceremony or formality . . . would be confined within the cell, a scorching fire would be encouraged in the monster stove adjoining, into which vegetable matter, old bones, pieces of rubber shoes and kindred trophies would be thrown, all to make a terrible heat, offensive as it was hot, to at last become so torturous and terrible as to cause the sickened and perspiring object of punishment to reveal the innermost secrets he possessed as compensation for release from the "sweat box."

Decades later, such methods had been mostly eliminated from police work—eliminated by new laws as well as by changing cultural standards. But during the 1960s, the Supreme Court responded to the demands and challenges of the civil rights movement through a series of new rulings. In *Mapp v. Ohio*, the court took the 50-year-old federal "exclusionary rule" and definitively extended its applicability to state trials. The exclusionary rule disallowed the use of illegally obtained evidence in criminal trials. The details of the 1961 case read like a scene from a movie. In May of 1957, three Cleveland police officers went to the home of a woman named Dollree Mapp and demanded entrance. They were operating on a tip that Mapp was harboring a suspect in a bombing that had occurred three days earlier. On advice from her lawyer, Mapp refused to admit the police without a search warrant. The officers came back three hours later with a number of reinforcements and a piece of paper that they claimed—falsely, as one of the officers would admit years afterward—was a warrant. They forced their way into the house, but found no bombing suspect. They did find some pornography (illegal at the time) and some illegal gambling paraphernalia and arrested Mapp. After being convicted and having her conviction upheld by the Ohio Supreme Court, Mapp took her case to the U.S. Supreme Court. The court overturned Mapp's conviction, ruling that the police had conducted an illegal search and seizure. The phony search warrant had been for a bombing suspect, not for the unrelated items that were eventually used to prosecute Mapp.

Two other cases in the 1960s helped to define the guidelines and rules under which all contemporary police officers operate—although one of these actually expanded, rather than limited, police prerogatives. In the 1968 case *Terry v. Ohio*, the Supreme Court ruled that if a police officer has reasonable suspicion that a person may be armed and dangerous, or about to commit a crime, the officer may stop that person and frisk him or her without violating the person's constitutional rights. In other words, the police may conduct a limited search of the person's outer clothing for weapons, regardless of whether the officer has probable cause for arrest. This stop-and-frisk ruling exists for the sole purpose of protecting police officers from attack. A cop who finds a bag of marijuana on a suspect during a frisk, for example, is not allowed to arrest the person for drug possession. Why not? A bag of marijuana, soft and spongy, is clearly not a weapon that could be used against the officer.

Supreme Court justice Byron White helped establish the "defense of life" standard for the police use of deadly force. Officers are now permitted to use deadly force only if a suspect is armed and dangerous or if there is probable cause to believe that the suspect has already seriously harmed someone.

The results of the landmark case *Miranda v. Arizona* (1966) are well known to anyone who's ever seen a cop TV show or movie. In this case, the Supreme Court determined that when criminal suspects are taken into police custody, they must be informed of their Fifth Amendment right against self-incrimination, their right to remain silent, and their Sixth Amendment right to an attorney.

As the police historians Bryan Vila and Cynthia Morris have pointed out, the Miranda warning is well known to most people today through its constant use by Hollywood scriptwriters. But the Court's ruling in *Miranda* "was highly controversial at the time. On the one hand, police officers feared it would hamper their efforts to investigate crimes and gain convictions, and many conservatives agreed. On the other hand, many liberals felt it was an important measure for enforcing citizens' constitutional rights and curbing police pressure."

In reality, though *Miranda* has changed the way police operate, it hasn't completely hamstrung their investigations, as opponents feared. "Police officers," one writer correctly points out, "found it easy to go through the motions of *Miranda* and still get suspects to confess." Still, the ruling had become controversial again by early 2000. Today's far more conservative Supreme Court may be willing to entertain arguments that the *Miranda* ruling places an undue burden on police officers and allows thousands of dangerous criminals to go free.

In the 1980s, another landmark Supreme Court case, *Tennessee v. Garner*, limited the police's right to use deadly force to apprehend suspected felons. (Felons are, by legal definition, those who commit serious crimes punishable by more than one year's imprisonment.) An old common law rule—borrowed from the English system, as is so much of American law—permitted police officers to use deadly force if necessary to catch any fleeing felon, no matter whether he or she posed a threat to the officers or bystanders. Vila and Morris explain: "This 'fleeing felon' rule was first established in England during the Middle Ages. It made more sense at the time, when all felonies were punishable by death anyway, and apprehending fleeing criminals was much more difficult once they were out of sight due to limited weapons and communications technology."

In America circa 1970–1980, the rule stopped seeming sensible, since police had many more options available to them for capturing criminals, especially those who didn't appear to be armed or dangerous. The issue came before the Supreme Court in 1985. In Tennessee, the police had shot and killed a 15-year-old, unarmed boy named Edward Garner as he was fleeing from a house he'd broken into. It was later determined he'd taken $10 and a purse. Garner's father sought damages against the police for violating his son's constitutional rights, but the state court defeated the case by citing the fleeing felon rule. An appeals court overturned the decision and ruled in favor of Mr. Garner, but then the state of Tennessee took its argument to the Supreme Court. The decision, delivered by Justice Byron White, was in favor of Garner, and the Court established the "defense of life" standard for police use of deadly force. This meant that officers were now permitted to use deadly force only if the suspect was armed and dangerous, or if there was probable cause to believe the suspect had committed a crime involving serious physical harm to somebody. These standards are still in effect today.

One of the many personal, occupational hazards of police work is the deep cynicism that can develop when officers witness the failures and inadequacies of the criminal justice system—a huge wheel in which they are only the first cog. In the face of so many Supreme Court rulings limiting their instincts and training, many officers come to distrust the system, feeling that it focuses on technical and procedural matters more than the fact of a person's innocence or guilt. "This experience borders on the twilight zone for some officers," Doerner writes. He then relates a typical anecdote from an officer who was almost killed in a confrontation with an armed suspect. Although the cop withheld fire, he was later accused of using excessive force and stealing money from the suspect's wallet. Eventually he got a disheartening phone call from the prosecutor, who

> advised me that he was dropping the charges. Dropping them! My blood boiled. Why? The voice at the other end . . . went on to explain that the state was dropping all charges and, in return, the defendant was dropping the allegations of police brutality and larceny. According to the voice, it was an expedient deal. Incredulous, I frothed and foamed, but the state attorney was not swayed. I went from a situation where I had ample probable cause to kill the man to being in the position of defending myself from an assailant's accusations and lost! I was shattered.

The problem with such situations is not limited to the fact that they tend to engender a cynical, jaded police force. A strong mistrust of the workings of official justice may also inspire police to take matters into their own hands. Doerner quotes one veteran street cop who puts the point unashamedly: "I never did feel bad about being violent, because the only people that I committed violence upon were people where that would be the only way they would get their justice. There is no justice in the justice system. You heard it before, they called it street justice. If you book a guy for robbery, if you can kick his ass, if you can make him pay for his crime, that would be the only place, right there on the street, because when he gets to court he's going to be dressed up, he's going to be clean-shaven, he's going to be talking nice to the judge."

In such cases, a hardened, violent, overzealous police officer risks becoming no better than the cruel and arbitrary vigilante groups of yore—proving once again that the good cop/bad cop paradigm remains with us, even at this late date in American law enforcement history.

Dark Side of the Force

No nation whose paid agents were lawless, and trampled upon public and individual rights, ever had anything but a disorderly people and a serious problem of smoldering rebellion and crime. . . .

    Citizens must suffer the effects of whatever hatred and antagonism against our public institutions may be bred by the departures of our police from constitutional justice and law.

—Ernest Jerome Hopkins, author of
Our Lawless Police (1931)

ighty years ago police officers had virtually no training. The police sometimes engaged in vigilantism and punished suspects themselves if they could not gather sufficient incriminating evidence to ensure justice in a court of law. During the anti-Communist Palmer Raids that took place after the end of World War I, many people suspected of being anarchists or Communists were rounded up by police and quickly deported. Instead of taking this "Communist" before a court of law, police have punished him themselves by placing him in stocks painted with the message, "This is for traitors."

New Yorkers, Los Angelenos, and other U.S. citizens today may feel that they have a lot to complain about when it comes to the police. But when contemporary individuals and communities speak out against police corruption, ineptitude, or brutality—issues that often dominate current domestic news—they may not be aware of just how old their complaints are. The state of American law enforcement 80 years ago was truly abysmal, and problems like graft or use of excessive force were arguably much more widespread than they are today. Despite the aspirations of progressive reformers like Vollmer and Wilson, police agencies around the country were poorly run. There was, as we have already learned, virtually no training for new officers. It was a commonly accepted practice for the police to wring confessions from suspects using "the third degree"—torture, beatings, sleep deprivation, starvation, psychological trickery, and other coercive techniques reminiscent of wartime or of religious inquisitions.

During the 1920s and 1930s under President Calvin Coolidge and then President Herbert Hoover, the federal government responded to the country's growing crime problem by forming a fact-finding committee (the Wickersham Committee) and issuing a number of studies on the status of the criminal justice system. Its 1931 report on the police included much troubling information about mismanagement and incompetence in law enforcement. Interpreting the results of the report, a writer named Ernest Jerome Hopkins published a book called *Our Lawless Police* shortly thereafter. In it, he argued that graft, brutality, and other bad behavior by the police had only served to increase the crime problem by destroying the public's trust in law enforcement. "Business men," Hopkins wrote, "will not confide to the police the names of the racketeers who prey upon them. Witnesses to gangster-shootings turn the other way and tell the police they have seen nothing. Much crime goes unreported because the victims have the intuitive feeling that the police do not represent the law but have become an irresponsible and unpredictable force."

As the police began to feel more helpless in the face of a rising tide of crime, Hopkins argued, they resorted to more desperate and violent measures—eliciting confessions using the third degree, and in some cases resorting to vigilantism and punishing a suspect them-

selves if they could not gather sufficient incriminating evidence to ensure justice in a court of law. This behavior only served to decrease the public's trust in and support of police actions. "So lawlessness begets more lawlessness, and the situation shows a vicious circle," Hopkins concluded.

Reforms in the 1940s and 1950s helped make substantial progress against the perennial problems of corruption and inefficiency, and several Supreme Court rulings helped put an end to the routine use of coercion and illegal searches and seizures by overzealous police officers. But by the late 1960s, other tensions between police and civilians had emerged. The civil rights and

The civil rights demonstrations of the 1950s and 1960s created tension between mostly white working-class police officers, the protesters, and citizens on both sides of the issue.

Demonstrators against the Vietnam War burn their draft cards on the steps of the Pentagon. Police and protesters often fought in the streets over the war; among the angry youth of the era, "pig" was the preferred label for a police officer.

anti-Vietnam movements called into question the entire social structure of the United States, particularly with regard to relatively powerless racial minorities, women, and working-class people. Individual police officers were still, for the most part, people from working-class backgrounds, and yet in their official roles they were the most visible symbol of established social authority—and therefore, from the point of view of protesters and demonstrators, agents of oppression. Among the angry youth of the era, "pig" was the preferred label for a police officer.

These years saw many mass demonstrations and protests mounted by African Americans who wanted the federal government and the states to enforce con-stitutional guarantees of racial equality. Although many of these protests followed the prescriptions for nonviolent civil disobedience recommended by Rev. Martin Luther King Jr. (who had been inspired by Gandhi and Thoreau), other actions were actually designed to gain publicity specifically by provoking a violent response from the police. To complicate matters, many of these protests were staged in direct response to incidents of alleged police brutality—proving, in effect, that Hopkins's vicious circle was still operating nearly half a century later.

Several reforms were instituted in the late 1960s and early 1970s to try to heal the rift between law enforcement and citizens. These included the establishment of independent review boards to handle citizen complaints and programs to recruit, hire, and promote more minority police officers (without tokenism and without segregating black cops in black neighborhoods), as well as efforts to decrease verbal and physical discourtesy by police officers and to ensure that cops worked as hard to fight crime in underprivileged areas as in wealthy districts. But while many of these programs and improvements did work as intended, it is clear even 20 to 25 years later that antagonisms between police and civilians continue to flare up on a regular basis.

Perhaps this is only to be expected. As we have already seen, for a large part of our early history, Americans resisted the notion of an official police force, perceiving it to be a way of giving the government too much power over ordinary citizens. But as communities grew too large to police themselves, it became necessary to empower agents to do so. However, once they've been empowered, such agents are no longer under the complete control of the communities that willed them into existence. They are our employees, but they are also in some ways our "bosses." This is an essential paradox that can be managed poorly or managed well, but never quite eliminated. Police work is, by its very nature, a coercive endeavor. Criminals generally must be found and brought to justice against their will. That is why, even if antagonisms between races, classes, and generations disappeared tomorrow, law-abiding citizens would still

The L.A. riots of 1992 were the worst riots in U.S. history. They started after four white police officers were acquitted in the beating of black motorist Rodney King. Here, two looting suspects are handcuffed as a police officer covers them with a shotgun.

sometimes suffer the consequences of having a police presence in their midst.

Consider, for example, the problem of excessive force. What exactly is it? Although police work may not be the deadliest occupation in the world—farm workers, firefighters, and construction workers all suffer higher mortality and injury rates—it is the only peacetime occupation in which you must prepare every day to kill or be killed. Police officers must be allowed the use of force so that they can protect themselves and do their jobs. But how much is too much? There are laws and guidelines that govern the use of force, but these theoretical rules often break down in practice, even among officers with the best training and the best intentions. And not all officers have had the best training or the best intentions.

The videotaped beating of Rodney King by LAPD officers in 1991 was perhaps the most widely publicized incident involving the use of excessive force in modern history. According to a commission report, King was driving over 100 miles an hour on a San Fernando Valley freeway when he was spotted by California Highway Patrol officers. A high-speed chase ensued, and King continued to speed and ran a stop sign and a red light before finally pulling over. It remains unclear whether King initially resisted arrest or obeyed police orders, but it is fairly clear from the videotape—made by a local resident who happened to witness the event—that the officers used far more force than necessary to subdue King. They hit him 56 times with batons over the course of about a minute and a half. This incident, made public soon thereafter, rekindled a long-standing debate over the LAPD's methods, particularly in relation to African-American men such as King. LAPD chief Daryl Gates had continued to use William H. Parker's war on crime style of management, and many people argued that excessive force was an inevitable outcome of this attitude. In the King beating, four white police officers were charged with excessive force, but then acquitted by a mostly white jury in April 1992. Los Angeles erupted into a six-day riot reminiscent of the disturbances of the 1960s. Fifty-two people were killed, 16,000 people were arrested, and almost $1 billion worth of property was destroyed. The relationship between the police and minority communities in Los Angeles continued to deteriorate.

At the time, reasonable people disagreed vehemently about the Rodney King incident, and may disagree still— a noteworthy fact, considering that this was a fairly clear-cut case that had the great advantage of being caught on tape. Other incidents are usually not so clear. Consider the situation of Frank Dwyer, a veteran of the New York

A somber moment at the funeral of a police officer killed in the line of duty. Although statistically other careers are more dangerous, police work is the only peacetime occupation in which a person might have to kill or be killed on any day.

force, who once had to subdue a man he witnessed breaking into a parked Jeep with a screwdriver. Dwyer was off-duty and dressed in plain clothes (although he was carrying a revolver), so he had called the local precinct for a car, which had not arrived yet. He decided he had to do something before the suspect took off, so he walked up to the Jeep and said, "Police, don't move. Stay in there." Although the suspect dropped his screwdriver at Dwyer's request, he then lunged at Dwyer and the two started grappling on the sidewalk. The man was reaching for Dwyer's gun, so the officer grabbed hold of it and brought the gun down hard on the man's head. Although blood was spurting from the suspect's head, he lunged yet again at Dwyer and managed to grab the cylinder of the gun.

The situation was desperate. "Should I shoot him?" Dwyer wondered, exhausted, fighting the man's drug-induced strength. Something held Dwyer back, and he raised his eyes for an instant, catching a brief glimpse of faces, people suddenly materialized in a circle around him, watching the struggle. Their expressions were tense, frightened, uncertain.

"I'm a police officer," Dwyer yelled. "Call the police. I need help!"

An experienced and judicious veteran, Dwyer had done his utmost to refrain from using deadly or excessive force against this suspect. He was not a "rogue cop," he was not the overzealous soldier in some desperate war on crime, but a good, responsible, thoughtful officer who'd witnessed a crime in progress. As a perverse reward for doing his duty, he, too, would be subject to the apparently never-ending mistrust between law enforcement and civilians. Backup had finally arrived and arrested the suspect (who would eventually end up in Bellevue, a hospital for the criminally insane, for observation before being booked for his crime). In the immediate aftermath, a waitress came out of a nearby restaurant and started talking to Dwyer. She didn't recognize him as the officer who'd been involved in the incident.

> "Isn't it terrible?" she said.
> "What?"
> "That every time the police catch somebody, they beat them up." Infuriated, Officer Dwyer explained what happened. "Well, I hope so," she said sarcastically, clearly skeptical, then walked away.

We will now take a look at some of the ways in which police have tried to regain or reinforce the trust of the citizenry, as well as the ways communities have tried to manage law enforcement, define norms of police behavior, and strike a healthier balance between themselves and their paid protectors. We will consider the possible long-term solutions to Hopkins's vicious circle of lawlessness in America. But before moving forward, there is another dark aspect to law enforcement that must be considered.

Police work exacts a heavy personal price from the men and women who do it. Each year, countless numbers of officers face assailants armed with guns, knives, or other weapons. Each year, dozens of officers around the country are killed in the line of duty. But although these losses are deeply mourned by families and communities, they represent a relatively small proportion of law enforcement. The hazards and the potential for death are there for all street officers, but the vast majority who survive those perils are often casualties of a different sort. As William G. Doerner writes,

> Officers who complete a tour of duty in one piece are not always fortunate enough to be spared from their share of human anguish. Imagine the emotional toll that officers feel when they must notify families that a loved one, either a parent or a child, is no longer alive. Other officers investigate child abuse incidents. There they see marks of unimaginable torture and demented violence perpetrated against children too little to understand why. Police personnel respond to wrecks where they try to rescue innocent people savagely maimed by irrational drunk drivers. They administer CPR in a futile effort to revive the lifeless stranger in their arms. They walk dark streets

Earning Your Street Degree, Part 1

In the late 1980s, a Chicago journalist named Connie Fletcher was able to gain access to the closed society of the police, in part because her sister was an officer in Area Six (a section of Chicago that includes the poorest ghettoes and the richest old-money neighborhoods), in part because she promised anonymity to the cops who would be willing to talk to her. She was able to interview 125 officers at great length over the course of several years, and the result was her groundbreaking, fiercely funny, somewhat horrifying, and endlessly fascinating book called *What Cops Know*. The police interviews shed light on the only credential that counts for an officer—the street degree—the practical knowledge built, each and every shift, through intimate encounters with crime, criminals, and the more extreme aspects of human nature.

All of Fletcher's interviewees were veterans of Area Six—some of the worldliest street cops in the country.

The cops who work the street are the first on any scene, whether they're the beat cars, responding to in-progress calls or situations, or the tac [tactical] officers, who work plainclothes, crime patterns, and in-progress calls. Beat and tac officers are called "the real police," a cop term edged with contempt for police who have bypassed the street. As one Area Six cop puts it: "A lot of the guys who have risen to the top never left the building. They're not the real police. Nobody should get to the top ranks who hasn't worked the street. Unless you've felt that trickle of sweat running down your back when you're running up and down stairs in the projects, unless you've felt that terror you get when you sense something horrible is about to happen, you're not the real police."

Veteran street cops have some amazing stories to tell. One of the Area Six cops told Fletcher about the night when he and his partner encountered a man with a knife sticking out of the top of his head.

All we could see was the hilt coming out. "Somebody stabbed me." "Okay, get in, get in, we'll take you to the hospital." He sat in the back of the squad [car]; he had to keep his head tilted so he wouldn't hit the car roof. The amazing and alleyways filled with the stench of garbage and the aroma of alcoholics, addicts, and other street people. Then they go home.

Policing is arguably one of the most physically and emotionally stressful jobs in the world. To handle that stress, many officers turn to alcohol to numb their feelings and block out the terrible memories. Young officers in particular seem to gravitate toward the bottle immediately after a harrowing experience—thereby establishing a pattern of dependency that may be very difficult or impossible to break out of years down the road. Drinking also helps alleviate the feelings of isolation

thing was, he was talking away, laughing, joking, didn't seem hurt at all. Perfectly calm. He just couldn't sit normally. We take him the hospital—he's out of the car, walks in, he's still talking to us normally.

They take him into surgery. We ask one of the docs, "Is he gonna make it?" The doc said, "The minute they take it out, he's dead." Just like that.

I don't know, I'd keep it in. Get a good barber.

Area Six, Fletcher was told, doesn't have the most homicides of any part of Chicago, but it has some of the most bizarre. During her interviews, she heard many stories about headless torsos, mutilated bodies, faces and skulls savaged by knife blade or blunt heavy objects. Faced with so much horrible bloodletting, most cops start to develop a real sense of gallows humor—a coarse, comedic response to all the death and destruction around them.

There is a torso that is found over in the Eighteenth District, in like a truck park. That's all it is—no arms, no legs, no head—just a torso. It has a shirt tucked around it.

The beat officers see this thing, and they don't know what it is. . . . So they call the homicide detectives and everything. The detective gets over there, and the beat officer goes, "Listen, I don't know what I got here. I'm not sure what it is. It *could* be a pig."

The homicide [detective] looks at the torso, and sees that it's got a tie on, around the neck of the shirt. He looks at the beat officer and says, "Kid, pigs don't wear neckties."

For cops who work homicides, deadpan humor may be the only way to relieve the unimaginable stress and horror of the job. "You can't work Homicide without changing," said one detective. "Once you've walked into a room and had something fall on your head, and it's a piece of . . . brain matter . . . that dropped from the ceiling, you just don't go out to dinner that night and chat with your pals."

and loneliness that officers feel when they do shift-work—that is, when their schedules are constantly changing from day shifts to night shifts, making it impossible for them to connect with family and friends in a consistent way. "Alcohol use is an occupationally sanctioned coping mechanism that officers use to decompress," Doerner writes. "However, continued abuse can lead to other problems. One survey showed that a quarter of the officers reported consuming a daily minimum dosage of three drinks."

Suicide is strikingly common among police officers. The constant exposure to human suffering and atrocities eventually takes its toll. More police officers die each year by their own hand than at the hands of criminals. (Of course, there may be complicating factors for why cops seem to kill themselves at a higher rate than the general population. For one thing, they have easy access to firearms and are trained in their use.)

Divorce rates are also extremely high, as a textbook on policing makes clear:

> One opening remark that some academy instructors use when they broach the topic of domestic life is very illustrative. The instructor tells the recruits to look at the person sitting to the left and at the one sitting to their right. Then the instructor drops the bomb, making the announcement in a hushed tone. Two out of every three persons sitting in the recruit class will get a divorce or a separation from their spouses over the next three years.

Only recently have police administrators begun to recognize the heavy toll that stress takes on their officers and to offer remedies such as counseling, fixed (non-rotating) shifts, and better access to exercise and physical training (a healthier way than alcohol to burn off stress). But these techniques are only in response to a tough job that will *always* be a tough job. This is what one veteran officer had to say on the matter:

I would not trade my experiences as a cop for anything in the world despite all the attendant heartaches. At the same time, I pray that my child will not grow up and swear the same oath. . . . When I see the bright faces and hear the lofty goals of new recruits fresh from the academy, a sense of ambivalence overwhelms me. I respect their enthusiasm for their new occupation but, at the same time, I pity the poor bastards.

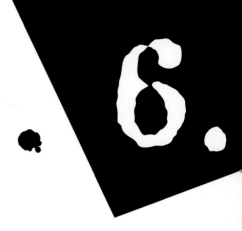

KINDER, GENTLER COPS?

> Given the awesome and complex nature of the police function, it follows that designing the arrangements and the organization to carry it out is equally complex. . . . We should not, therefore, lose patience because we have not yet come up with the perfect model; we should not get stalled trying to simplify change just to give uniform meaning to a single, catchy, and politically attractive term.
>
> —Herman Goldstein, in
> *The New Policing: Confronting Complexity* (1993)

I n the 1980s, the concept of community policing came to the fore once again in discussions about how to solve the "police problem." Ideas related to community-oriented law enforcement had been around, in one form or another, at least since the time

The concept of community policing encourages police officers to become peacekeepers and community service professionals, thereby winning citizens' trust. But some critics have viewed this model as nothing more than a trendy phrase.

of August Vollmer and his notion of police as social workers. In 1979, law professor Herman Goldstein argued for something he called problem-oriented policing, which would obligate officers to identify, define, analyze, and solve specific problems in a community (such as muggings, house burglaries, domestic violence, and so on) instead of simply responding to calls and solving crimes that had already taken place. By the late 1980s, many cities and towns across the United States had put such concepts into practice, by establishing or expanding foot patrols, improving communications

Earning Your Street Degree, Part 2

To read the real stories from the mouths of cops is to have many of your TV- and movie-inspired misconceptions corrected. "Ever see on TV where the police car pulls up to the scene of the crime with the siren going? The cops jump out? Now that's completely absurd," says one cop interviewed by writer Connie Fletcher. "If you want to *catch* the fellow, you're gonna turn your siren off a couple of blocks away." At the same time, you start to realize that cops are human, not the clear-cut heroes or villains of fiction. And some of them are guilty of the same kinds of mundane laziness or incompetence that might afflict a computer programmer or car salesman. "There's a lot of policemen who will have their sirens going on all the way up to the front of the place because they *want* the guy to get away. They don't want the paperwork. They don't want to go to court." In other words, they're avoiding doing the very job they're paid to do: arresting suspects.

Another fictional misconception that cops will set you straight on, if given a chance: the ubiquitous idea that criminals are somehow smarter than ordinary, law-abiding citizens. If anything, the opposite is most likely the case. Somebody, for example, murdered a man and left him headless, legless, and armless in a truck park. But that same somebody neglected to check his victim's shirt pocket. Although he'd gone to all that trouble to keep the victim from being identified, he hadn't noticed the man's business card tucked into his shirt pocket. "I tell you what. If offenders ever got bright, we'd be in a world of trouble," said one of the Area Six veterans. Another cop interviewed by Fletcher talked about how easy it is for homicide officers to "clear" (solve) investigations. Murderers do stupid things like taking evidence from the scene or keeping the murder weapon with them. Most murderers are known to their victims— if not intimately known, at least fairly well acquainted. "It's seldom the kind of premeditated, involved, complicated thing like you read in Agatha Christie," he said.

Cops who specialize in particular departments come to see certain patterns in the way crimes "go down." They come to have certain stock beliefs about the way criminals behave. Homicide detectives between the police and the public, setting up shop-front police stations in communities, establishing Neighborhood Watch programs, and creating liaisons between the police and minority groups.

In community policing paradigms, the officer's roles as peacekeeper and community service professional were supposed to eclipse his or her traditional job as law enforcer. But such a paradigm always had to compete with a more authoritarian, conservative approach—the legacy of William Parker's "war against crime" philosophy. Under both President Ronald

know that serial killers are extremely personable, while mass murderers are not. Although there may be some notable exceptions to this rule, there are tons of cases that confirm it again and again. Undercover narcotics cops know that greed will usually override a drug dealer's suspicions: He may suspect you're a cop, but in the heat of the moment, with the possibility of making a nice tidy sum from the drug transaction, he'll risk it anyway. Property crimes specialists know the difference between "good burglars"—those who plan and execute large scores with deliberation and finesse—and "s—head burglars"—drug addicts turned into felons because of their need for cash. Cops on the organized crime beat know that two of the current biggest moneymakers for mobsters are pornographic video rentals and dollar peep shows. As Fletcher notes in her book *What Cops Know:*

> Cops know things other people don't. They know that most murderers want to confess. They know that child molesters sometimes marry single women with kids for the sole purpose of molesting those kids when they reach the right age. Cops know that the biggest day of the year for Gypsy thieving is Good Friday. They know that the person who discovers a murder victim is usually the murderer, and that many rapists expect their victims to fall in love with them. They know that most mob hitmen like to borrow the victim's car trunk to avoid dirtying up their own. They know that the best con is the simplest con and that whores know more about what's going on in the street than anyone.

Witnessing all this bad behavior—from the shabby and deceitful to the downright evil—experienced cops can't help but grow jaded about human nature. But it's a big mistake for police officers to start to believe they've seen it all and can handle everything. As one of Connie Fletcher's interviewees put it, "You never stop learning. You never get your street degree. The person who says they have their street degree or they've learned it all is the person that's going to wind up either dead or in a very compromising position. They've closed their minds. They're gonna wind up having a problem."

Reagan and his successor, George Bush, a major theme of the newly ascendant conservative ideology was the belief that governments and public agencies should behave more like private corporations. In their new focus on the "bottom line," police agencies started to pay a lot of attention to crime statistics as a measure of police performance. This put pressure on officers to behave primarily as law enforcers rather than as social workers, community liaisons, service professionals, or any of the other possible roles they might have played. In this atmosphere, the notion of community policing came to be seen as a sham, at least by some critics—"a trendy phrase spread thinly over customary reality" was how one leading police scholar described it. Furthermore, the pressure to reduce crime statistics by any means necessary seemed to create a great temptation or incentive for officers to cross the line from good cop to bad cop—to once again resort to excessive force (as in the Rodney King incident) and antagonistic behavior against ordinary citizens.

Los Angeles police chief William H. Parker was a proponent of the "war on crime" philosophy of policing. Critics argue that such an approach creates tension between citizens and police, which can in turn lead to misunderstandings and violence.

By 1990, it was clear that the police were being expected to do too many things all at once, to play too many conflicting roles simultaneously. As a national task force report stated succinctly that year, "The policeman lives on the grinding edge of social conflict, without a well-defined, well-understood notion of what he is supposed to be doing there."

These conflicting expectations of police were contributing to yet another problem: the deepening of the so-called blue wall of silence, a code of loyalty among cops that keeps them from reporting each other's wrongdoings. In the mid-1990s, police historian Bryan Vila looked into this problem and came to believe that the code of silence was not some unchanging fact of police life, but a fixable problem. "The tendency of police to protect one another is a natural response by people who routinely try to meet unrealistic demands in extraordinarily difficult situations," he asserted.

> Take the case of the normally diligent and professional officer who erupts and strikes that one person too many who screams in his face at the end of an arduous night. Acting out of anger rather than fear for his safety, he has committed a felony. If he is truthful, the career that defines him is over. He could go to prison. If he chooses to lie, he must obtain his partner's complicity. They both knew he was wrong, but they also know that any person who repeatedly dealt with the same situation would blow it eventually. Recognizing that the system makes impossible demands and offers impossible choices, they choose to submit a false report and, if necessary, perjure themselves.

Vila argued that "if we could control the unreasonable expectations that allow officers to justify their failure to police one another, we might eliminate much of the actual and perceived police misconduct that cripples our ability to control crime." For example, the unrealistic expectation that cops, rather than communities, control crime "increases the zeal with which many officers approach their job. When one participates in a crusade, it is easy to rationalize extreme measures."

Vila, who was a cop before he became a historian, did more than make philosophical pronouncements—he offered practical solutions. Primarily he suggested a rethinking of the way police officers' shifts are usually handled, especially for cops in high-crime areas, who may have to work through "several adrenaline-pumping incidents a shift" and will probably be doing so while exhausted from overtime assignments, off-duty court appearances, and other job-related activities. "We limit the amount of time pilots, truck drivers, and medical interns work, yet tolerate chronically fatigued cops," Vila complained.

While Vila made suggestions aimed at eroding the blue wall of silence and bringing public expectation in line with the actual work police could do, other thinkers were also reviewing the recent history of American law enforcement and asking fundamental questions: What exactly should the police be charged with doing? What responsibilities are rightfully theirs? How exactly should public expectations of police work be revised? An unexpected and controversial response to these questions came from David Bayley, author of *Police for the Future* (1994). Although crime prevention had typically always been considered an important part of police work, Bayley had studied the research and found that there is no "connection between the number of police officers and crime rates" and that "the primary strategies adopted by modern police have been shown to have little or no effect on crime."

The upshot of this somewhat shocking conclusion was that "we cannot rely upon the police, even when they are dedicated to preventing crime, to save society from crime. No single institution can do that." And yet, Bayley admitted, the police are indeed the best candidates to take the lead in fighting and preventing crime. But to do it would require a complete revision of policing institutions.

> It will require policing to be demilitarized. Policing must no longer be viewed as a war, dominated by the use of force devised by senior ranks and carried out by "troops" whose primary duty is obedience. Policing will need to be stood on its head. In conventional policing, the assessment of needs and the development of strategies are done at the top, by senior staff. Lower echelons carry out the plans that headquarters formulate. In order for crime to be prevented effectively, responsibility for diagnosing needs and formulating action plans must be given to frontline personnel.

Bayley's suggestion that we "demilitarize" police harks back, of course, to the very roots of American law enforcement history. The early European settlers of the

American colonies were in some sense quite right to fear and mistrust the idea of a "standing army" in their midst, a permanent police force given the power of life, death, and freedom over ordinary citizens. It is clear that our complex, crowded, and violent society certainly requires some form of law enforcement. It is also clear that police officers require power in order to do their jobs. Giving cops too little real power to effect justice only serves to create a disgruntled police force prone to brutality and vigilantism. But history also reveals the problems that can arise in the opposite case, if the police are given too much power, as were the Regulators. So exactly how much power should be given, and to whom, and over whom, and with what limitations and restrictions? These are provisional questions that will never be answered in the absolute. Instead, they will have to be asked again and again, so that the answers have some hope of staying relevant in a dynamically growing and changing society such as ours.

Even if police departments adopt more community-friendly approaches, history suggests that some degree of tension will always exist between the police and the citizens over whom they exercise so much authority. Police departments are attempting to defuse these tensions by recruiting minorities. Here, an Asian-American man takes an application for the New York City Police Department.

Bibliography

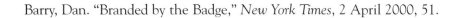

Barry, Dan. "Branded by the Badge," *New York Times*, 2 April 2000, 51.

Bayley, David. *Police for the Future*. New York: Oxford, 1994.

Doerner, William G. *Introduction to Law Enforcement: An Insider's View*. Englewood Cliffs, N.J.: Prentice-Hall, 1992.

Dulaney, W. Marvin. *Black Police in America*. Bloomington: Indiana University Press, 1996.

Fletcher, Connie. *What Cops Know: Cops Talk About What They Do, How They Do It, and What It Does to Them*. New York: Villard Books, 1991.

Gellman, Stuart. *Cops: The Men and Women Behind the Badge*. Tucson, Ariz.: Horizon Press, 1993.

Goldstein, Herman. *The New Policing: Confronting Complexity*. Washington, D.C.: National Institute of Justice, U.S. Department of Justice, 1993.

Hopkins, Ernest Jerome. *Our Lawless Police*. New York: Viking, 1931.

Leinen, Stephen. *Gay Cops*. New Brunswick, N.J.: Rutgers University Press, 1993.

MacDonald, Heather. "How to Train Cops," *City Journal* 10, no. 4 (Autumn 2000).

Prassel, Frank. *The Western Peace Officer*. Norman: University of Oklahoma Press, 1972.

Rachlin, Harvey. *The Making of a Cop*. New York: Pocket Books, 1991.

Ragonese, Paul, and Berry Stainback. *The Soul of a Cop.* New York, St. Martin's Press, 1991.

Skolnick, Jerome. *Justice Without Trial: Law Enforcement in Democratic Society.* New York: John Wiley & Sons, 1966.

Vila, Bryan, and Cynthia Morris. *The Role of Police in American Society: A Documentary History.* Westport, Conn.: Greenwood Press, 1999.

Index

Index

Index

Picture Credits

SANDY ASIRVATHAM is a graduate of Columbia University with a B.A. in Philosophy & Economics and an M.F.A. in Creative Writing. As a freelance writer and reporter, she has written extensively about business, government, and the arts. This is her first foray into the history and practice of law enforcement.

AUSTIN SARAT is William Nelson Cromwell Professor of Jurisprudence and Political Science at Amherst College, where he also chairs the Department of Law, Jurisprudence and Social Thought. Professor Sarat is the author or editor of 23 books and numerous scholarly articles. Among his books are *Law's Violence*, *Sitting in Judgment: Sentencing the White Collar Criminal*, and *Justice and Injustice in Law and Legal Theory*. He has received many academic awards and held several prestigious fellowships. In addition, he is a nationally recognized teacher and educator whose teaching has been featured in the *New York Times*, on the *Today* show, and on National Public Radio's *Fresh Air*.